TABLE OF CONTENTS

PART III:
MARGINALIZATION AND TRANSGRESSION IN MODERN FRENCH LITERATURE

ACKNOWLEDGEMENTS

The 2001 Group is an inter-university postgraduate community in French Studies under the direction of Professor Naomi Segal at the University of Reading; it is part of the Collaboration Programme in Modern Languages, funded by HEFCE under its Restructuring & Collaboration Fund and administered by the UCML and the Subject Centre in Languages, Linguistics and Area Studies. This, the first publication of the 2001 Group, would not have been possible without the external funding provided.

We are grateful to the University of Reading for hosting the publication workshop in March 2003 without charge, and to the participants for ensuring that the day was such a success. We would also like to thank Ann Lewis, a contributor to the volume, who kindly produced the original piece of artwork for the front cover of the book, and Mr. Marc Garanger who granted permission for his photographs to be reproduced free of charge. The editors would especially like to thank Professor Naomi Segal for her advice and and support throughout.

INTRODUCTION

This is the first publication of the 2001 Group, an inter-university postgraduate community in French Studies. One of the principal roles of the 2001 Group is to encourage exchanges between research students, and indeed this book brings together articles from postgraduates from around the world. Although devoted to the theme of the forbidden, the publication was in fact produced in a spirit of open-minded collaboration. Our book is not so much peer-reviewed as peer-edited, the result of a publication workshop held at the University of Reading in March 2003, in which each contributor participated in the editing process of all the articles.

The articles collected here represent the diverse and interdisciplinary nature of current research by postgraduates in the notoriously broad field of French Studies. The title we have chosen - *Reading and Writing the Forbidden: Essays in French Studies* - indicates that the focus of our project is to explore the ways in which texts are circumscribed by forbidden territory. We use 'texts' here in a very broad sense, encompassing photography and film, as well as literary and non-literary written works. Reading the forbidden involves examining the constraints (aesthetic, linguistic, ideological, conceptual) which inevitably delimit all texts. However, it is also appropriate to talk of writing the forbidden, since texts are privileged sites for the articulation, and indeed the breaking, of taboos. All of the articles included here deal in one way or another with the curious nature of texts, which are both constrained by the forbidden, and transgress its limitations.

The advantage of a collection of articles on a single, broad theme is that it can, and must, embrace divergent perspectives and methods. This is the best way to approach the innumerable ways in which writing and reading the forbidden can be understood. The point is not to seek to develop a single, transcendent sense of the forbidden, which would be a hopeless task from the outset, but to explore a few of the ways in which notions of reading and writing the forbidden shed light on French texts.

Study of the forbidden is bound to be sensitive to the historical context of textual production. What is forbidden to one time and place can be acceptable, even *de rigueur*, to another era. What was forbidden in the distant past may seem more easily recognizable than what is forbidden to us now. Nonetheless, in their conscious and unconscious articulation of what was forbidden to them, texts from the past are necessarily foreign to us. The fact that the category of the forbidden in past texts is both deceptively easy to identify and inevitably strange accounts for the large number of articles on early modern literature here, which make up almost half of the contributions to our book, and all of Part I. Julia Horn's article explores how the immense sixteenth-century chivalric romance, *Amadis de Gaule*, is bound by generic limitations which mean that certain events, particularly the death of the hero, are forbidden in the narrative. While Horn reads the forbidden in *Amadis*, Hugh Roberts looks at how early modern texts write the forbidden, through reference to the distant pagan past of the Cynics. The scandalous truth-telling of these ancient philosophers is used by writers, including Montaigne, to open up difficult and dangerous ideas. Marilyn Cox examines the ways in which Jean-Pierre Camus seeks to contain the forbidden acts described in his narration of horrifying *histoires tragiques* within a moralizing discourse, which sometimes seems to protest too much. The capacity of texts to broach material and ideas they expressly condemn is also explored by Ann Lewis, who argues that *La Nouvelle Héloïse* contains within it the seeds of a forbidden reverse-reading, which would have had Rousseau turning in his grave. Probably the most wantonly outrageous text examined here is the *Erotika Biblion* of the eighteenth-century *libertin*, Mirabeau. Isabelle Dotan-Robinet analyses the philosophical criteria that lie behind Mirabeau's defiance of taboos, and how his essay falls into both incoherence and unconscious expression of prejudice.

Plainly, however, the realm of the forbidden is not restricted to early modern texts. Part II focuses on how the forbidden is framed and frames photography and cinema. What should or should not be depicted on film is in an obvious sense a uniquely modern phenomenon. Nonetheless, revealing connections between text and image are as old as writing itself. The ways in which juxtapositions of text and image can illuminate the forbidden is an underlying theme of articles on such diverse texts as Rousseau's *La Nouvelle Héloïse*, the works of Pierre Loti, and the nineteenth-century right-wing political press in Paris. The latter's representation of the Commune, the memory of which it sought to mythologize and suppress, is the subject of Colette Wilson's contribution. Catherine Guy-Murrell draws on Barthes's writings on photography to illuminate the broaching of aesthetic and cultural taboos in photographing of veiled women in the twentieth and twenty-first centuries. The starting point of Libby Saxton's article is that the real is in a sense forbidden in filmic (and indeed textual) representation. However, Saxton argues that what is ontologically forbidden to film implies that some types of cinematic representation should be ethically forbidden.

Part III concentrates on the themes of transgression and marginalization in modern French literature. As Morag Young argues in her article, these two concepts are linked, since the transgressive person is invariably marginal. Using insights drawn from psychoanalysis, Peter Turberfield argues that Pierre Loti's apparently exploitative, and ostensibly forbidden, sexual treatment of 'Oriental' dress and individuals symbolically reverses the power relations between colonizer and colonized. Victoria Reid investigates how Gide tries to have his forbidden fruit and eat it by seeking to displace his transgressive sexuality onto predatory women. Joanna Shearer uses Kristeva's arguments concerning the 'abject' nature of women's bodies to provide a means of approaching Simone de Beauvoir's Le Sang des autres. Morag Young looks at how both literal and metaphorical border-crossing sheds light on the quest for identity as expressed in the novels of Duras, Modiano, and Darrieussecq. The search for identity both within and outside the constraints of the forbidden is a recurrent theme in the articles of Part III, whether it is Loti's search for a self through transvestism, Gide's exploration of his sexuality, or Beauvoir's attempt to frame the female body. The ways in which selves are fashioned with reference to forbidden frontiers mirrors the way in which texts are both constrained by, and transgress, the limits of the forbidden.

While our book is most obviously relevant to specialists in each of the areas covered by its three parts, it would also reward the reader on the look out for unexpected connections between articles devoted to very diverse subject-matter. Nothing is forbidden to the reader who is happy to see Rousseau rub shoulders with transvestites, Simone de Beauvoir in close company with macho eighteenth-century libertines, and The Matrix alongside Rabelais. For each of the contributors, writing the forbidden was a great opportunity to exchange ideas and to participate in unfamiliar areas of French Studies. Now we can only hope that reading the forbidden proves as enjoyable, informative, and liberating as writing the forbidden.

Hugh Roberts

PART I:
FORBIDDEN WRITINGS AND READINGS OF
EARLY MODERN FRENCH TEXTS

The *Histoires Tragiques*: Edification or Subversive Entertainment?

Marilyn Cox
Oxford Brookes University

In early-seventeenth-century France the very idea of 'fiction' was a contentious issue. As Erica Harth explains, *fable* and *nouvel* were not 'nice' words: 'They frequently carried the odor of "lies" and, perhaps more faintly, even of something slightly pornographic or at best scandalously titillating'.[1] Although the *romans sentimentaux* of Nervèze were taken to church by women who saw them as valuable adjuncts to instruction in social etiquette and pious behaviour, various volumes of *Amadis de Gaule*, much in demand at this time, regaled readers with tales of giants, magic, bloody battles, licentious behaviour and incredible happenings.[2] *Amadis* and works similar to it were condemned by those who feared that young and impressionable minds would be corrupted by seductive descriptions of adventurous escapades and illicit love. It was just such a concern that prompted François de Sales, Bishop of Geneva from 1602 until his death in 1629, to urge Jean-Pierre Camus (1584-1652), Bishop of Belley from 1609 to 1629, to employ his talents as a raconteur in producing a Christian alternative to these forbidden fruits.

When Camus embarked on this project, another form of literature, the *histoire tragique*, had been attracting a growing number of readers since the appearance of Boaistuau's and Belleforest's translation/adaptation of some of Bandello's more tragic tales (1560-1580). In particular, François de Rosset's *Histoires mémorables et tragiques de ce temps* (first edition 1614, extended by the author in 1619) had been a best-seller. The *histoire tragique*, like the still popular *histoire prodigieuse*, emphasized the extraordinary and cruel aspects of life, and frequently warned of the dire consequences of incurring God's wrath.[3] However, whereas the former dealt with extraordinary phenomena such as earthquakes, floods and monstrous births, interpreting these as Divine wrath inflicted on a wicked generation, the latter restricted itself to the remarkable effects of men's passions and ill fortune. Both could be considered a more sophisticated and enduring form of the *canards*, pamphlet literature bought in the streets for a few *sous* and soon discarded, whose popularity peaked around the time Rosset produced his collection of tragic tales.

Camus realized that this type of narrative was eminently suited to his own purpose and indeed acknowledged the influence of earlier authors: 'je marche après les pas de François de Belleforest et de François de Rosset, qui ont auparavant moi écrit des Histoires tragiques avec un succès assez heureux'.[4] However, such a venture was not without problems. In 1628, when Camus published his first collection of tragic tales, serious edification was still considered the domain of historians, who were reluctant to see their role usurped by authors of fiction. While *exempla* taken from Antiquity were considered legitimate vehicles for the transmission of a moral message, products of the imagination of contemporary authors were dismissed as 'lies', unworthy of such a role. Camus therefore took pains to assure his readers that the events he described were based on what could actually happen in real life. Even so, his graphic descriptions of the often bloody consequences of unrestrained passions laid him open to accusations of impropriety. The Council of Trent had condemned works presenting indecent ideas couched in elegant prose and consequently any salacious details of scandalous happenings were necessarily accompanied by vehement proclamations of a didactic intent. Lever maintains that even Camus used moralizing merely as an excuse for writing lurid tales: 'Sous prétexte de livrer un combat sans merci aux passions les plus dégradantes, il les décrit avec une complaisance à peine dissimulée'.[5]

However, despite the criticism levelled against him, it is hard to refute the sincerity of Camus's didactic intentions, not only because of his eminent ecclesiastical position but because of the evident pains he takes throughout his narrative to educate his readers with moralizing asides, metaphors, similes and biblical allusions. In contrast to this, Rosset's exaggerated expressions of outrage and theatrical posturing suggest that he is simply striking an attitude, knowing that his readers will interpret this as a reassurance that their expectation of horror will be satisfied. 'O temps! O siècle! O moeurs! Que les mortels sont dépravés!' he rails in the course of an account of homosexual rape, which offers the essential ingredients for a sensational tale: sex (and, moreover, deviant sex), the scandal of a corrupt monk, and a villainous but seemingly noble and generous *Chevalier de Malte*.[6] But the reader is clearly intended to enjoy the excitement of a protracted account of how the unsuspecting victim is stalked from town to town before being eventually lured into the monastery. Knutson's reference to Rosset's 'pretence of teaching a lesson' and 'eloquently trumpeted intentions' which do not match 'glib finales' is well justified.[7] A complicity is established between author and reader, tacitly acknowledging that although, for propriety's sake, both sides must maintain the pretence of a desire for moral improvement, the chief requirement is for entertainment.

Forbidden passions and their punishment

Whether or not the exhortations to lead virtuous lives were sincere, the sentiments of the *histoires tragiques* undoubtedly chimed with concerns expressed in popular philosophical works of the time. The neo-stoic philosophy propounded in Pierre Charron's *De la Sagesse* (1601), which still exerted significant influence in the 1620s, warned that any weakness in man's will that led to the understanding being overpowered by the senses would give free rein to 'tous les fols et seditieux de l'ame, qui sont les passions'.[8] Neo-stoic insistence on the need to discipline the will to prevent the evil effects of the passions persisted alongside the newer Christian humanism of François de Sales, Camus's mentor, whose *Introduction à la vie dévote* (1609) argued that, through the grace of God, the passions could be turned to good use and that sinners could be brought to repentence through the redemptive power of God's grace, rather than by fear. However, Camus does not display such confidence in the tractability of the passions and considered tales focusing on the horrors of divine retribution far more efficacious in correcting society's ills than those showing the good being rewarded: 'comme le monde est composé de plus de méchants que de bons, il est besoin de donner de la crainte et de la terreur à ceux-là par la vue des peines que les lois ordonnent et font souffrir à ceux qui s'écartent de leur devoir'.[9] In his tragic tales, avarice, overweening ambition and lust frequently drive characters to commit savage acts that ultimately lead to their ruin. His approach seems more akin to that of Cardinal Bérulle, a renowned preacher who died in 1629, who incited a fear of the devil and the punishments of hell in order to persuade the recalcitrant to amend their ways. Indeed, Camus considered this fear of the forbidden and of failure to resist temptation essential to spiritual health, declaring 'La seureté et confiance en soy est totalement dommageable et nuisible'.[10] He warned, too, of the dangers of insincere repentence: 'ce n'est pas assez de faire

Penitence, si on ne se repent comme il faut, car l'honneur du Roy de Gloire aime le iugement'.[11]

While emphasizing the need for self-discipline, particularly among the young, Camus was equally adamant that parents should not impose unreasonable constraints on their children. The disastrous effects of exerting undue pressure on a daughter to marry a rich suitor for whom she has no affection, or of opposing the marriage of a son or daughter into a family of lower rank, is a recurrent theme in his *histoires tragiques* – twelve of the fifty-four stories in *Les Rencontres funestes* are based on such a situation.[12] Prior to the Council of Trent, the Church did not require a formal ceremony or the approval of the parents of the bride and groom in order to consider a marriage binding in the sight of God.[13] However, as a result of the Edict of 1579, if a girl under twenty-five married without her parents' approval 'she was deemed to have been suborned into marriage, the union was termed clandestine, and her partner became liable to the death penalty', although this punishment was rarely applied.[14] Pressed by avaricious parents – the root cause of many a tragedy – to marry a rich suitor she did not love, a girl might elope with the man of her choice or engage in a *mariage clandestin*, that is, one entered into without parental consent. DiPiero suggests that the *histoires tragiques* showed that only love between a man and a woman who were socially compatible would be sanctioned, no matter how faithful or chaste the couple, and that they were written specifically to reinforce the social codes of the aristocracy.[15] However, although Camus does, indeed, advise the young not to rebel rashly against their parents' wishes, he emphasizes that there can be no justification for coercion as far as marriage is concerned, 'puis que l'essence de ce Sacrement consiste en l'vnion de deux franches volontez'.[16] And Rosset's story of Flaminie, whose father and mother arrange for her to marry the wealthy brother of a Cardinal 'sans s'informer si elle l'avait agréable', serves as a warning to all parents that 'tous les enfants ne sont pas d'un si bon naturel que de se conformer à leurs volontés'.[17]

According to Camus, together with sexual attraction, despair is the most dangerously deluding of all the passions: 'ces furieux démons […] traînent toujours ceux qui les suivent en des précipices horribles, et les portent à des fins tragiques et misérables'.[18] However, although he generally condemns suicide, the ultimate act of despair, which was condoned by supporters of neo-stoic doctrine and viewed sympathetically by Montaigne,[19] his attitude is more complex than outright censure on the basis of the sixth commandment. He deplores the action of an unmarried mother, who kills herself because she believes nobody will help her, declaring that she should have prayed for divine assistance, which would have inspired her to return to her father in the manner of the prodigal son.[20] Yet he does not criticize a young man intending become a monk, who inflicts mortal wounds on himself to avoid being seduced by the prostitute his father has engaged to deter him from his vocation. Instead, Camus confesses that here his own judgement leans 'plutôt à la louange qu'au blâme'.[21] It would appear that he condemns suicide in those who fail to turn to God for assistance but views it more sympathetically when it is deemed to be God's will because no other alternative has been provided for a virtuous character by divine intervention. In the case of the young man who mutilates his body, Camus comments that 'Dieu qui le voulait en sa part abrégea ses jours'.[22] Rosset's attitude is yet more lenient; he admires a woman who chooses to die with her lover rather than share the dishonour brought by his cowardly murder of a man he was to have fought in a duel. He describes her death as 'constante et généreuse' and remarkable at a time when 'Les dames y font profession de l'inconstance et à peine en trouverait-on une semblable en tout le monde'.[23]

Variations in the attitude of both Rosset and Camus towards vengeance, described by Charron as a 'passion lasche et effeminée, d'ame foible et basse, pressée et foulée',[24] further illustrate the subtleties of judgement found in the *histoires tragiques* regarding what is forbidden. Rosset begins *HM* XIV by denouncing vengeance for banishing reason but does not follow up his condemnation, as Charron does, with positive advice that those who are wronged should 'faire bouquer l'ennemy par bien-faits, et d'ennemy le rendre amy'.[25] Instead of championing Stoic restraint or Christian forgiveness, his story shows some sympathy for a woman who enjoys inflicting the most sadistic torture on the murderer of the man she loved, gouging out his eyes, cutting off his nose and ears, tearing out his teeth and nails, and removing his fingers one by one – all while he is still conscious. Far from condemning the woman's behaviour, the conclusion justifies her vicious acts: 'Il y en a néanmoins qui blâment quelquefois la grande cruauté qu'elle exerça sur Clorizande, mais quand ils viennent à considérer puis après sa juste douleur et sa perte, l'on met au rang de ces généreuses dames tant célèbres dans les histoires des Anciens' (p. 337). Camus's attitude, too, varies according to the particular crime involved. On the one hand, he advises against taking revenge, since inflamed passion leads men to mete out excessive punishments incompatible with the crime: 'Vne des raisons pourquoy Dieu s'est reserué la vengeance, c'est parce qu'estant sans passion il punit les fautes auec toute Iustice'.[26] Yet when telling how a girl is abducted and raped on her wedding day, he finds it acceptable that the rapist, even though he renounces the world and becomes a monk, should be murdered in his monastery by the man who had intended to marry the girl:

> il semble que la Iustice de Dieu ait permis ce mauuais effect pour apprendre aux criminels que s'ils ont violé sacrilegement vn sacrement, et honorable, et venerable, ce n'est ny des lieux, ny des habits sacrez qu'il doiuent faire leurs boucliers et leurs refuges, autrement la pieté se rendroit protectrice de son contraire.[27]

Although aware of the need to take circumstances into consideration when judging a person's actions, Camus shows little sympathy for unrepentent sinners but Rosset's attitude appears more worldly and pragmatic. Having denounced a man for attempting to seduce a married woman, he admires the courage he shows in fighting the woman's angry husband and his men: 'Que je plains l'injustice de ton sort! Tu devais mourir à la tête de quelque armée, pour la foi, pour ton roi et pour ta patrie!' (*HM* XXI, p. 457). And, while he does not condone the behaviour of a brother and sister due to be executed for their incestuous relationship, he adopts a sympathetic attitude towards them and exploits the emotional appeal of the events (*HM* VII).

As a bishop, Camus is concerned not only with what is forbidden by men but what is deemed sinful by God. In the introduction to *La Iustification criminelle* he states that, although man's justice may not always consider the intent as culpable as the deed, in cases where an attempt has been made to commit a crime the punishment must be the same as if the act had been actually carried out.[28] A Duke's servant is executed simply because he reveals that he might be susceptible to disloyalty that could endanger his master's life;[29] another man is executed after confessing under torture to a murder he did not commit, but the fact that he had wished the victim dead elicits Camus's comment that his execution may well have been the will of God 'qui ne punit pas seulement les effects mais les desirs'.[30]

The complexities of the moral message

Poli is adamant that Rosset conveys a subversive message supporting *libertin* views by portraying Jules-César Vanini, executed on 6 February 1619 for disseminating anti-Christian ideas, as a worthy person.[31] Poli suggests, for example, that Rosset endorses Vanini's forbidden teaching by adding to the original *canard* words allegedly spoken by a priest in support of the vilified man and by indicating that the court wished to spare him but was practically obliged to find him guilty.[32] But Rosset states explicitly that the court's wish was that Vanini should *repent* and be saved: 'Ce vénérable Sénat, curieux de sauver cette âme damnée, n'avait point envie de procéder à son juste jugement, sans avoir premièrement tâché de le réduire à salut' (*HM* V, p. 175). Moreover, the insertion of the priest's comments is offset by the addition of an equal number of words (about 500) *condemning* Vanini's opinions.[33] In this instance, therefore, rather than engaging in subversive propaganda, Rosset is simply raising the original account to a more literary level and providing supplementary material to exercise the reader's critical faculties. The authors of *histoires prodigieuses* would similarly often set out different views on controversial subjects before voicing their own opinions or electing to remain undecided, and *canardiers* might attempt to explain how unusual phenomena resulted from natural causes but then dismiss this possibility and assert that God was indeed giving a warning through these events.

However, at a time when free will, as opposed to the Calvinist belief in predestination, was such a fiercely defended aspect of Catholicism, it could, at first, seem surprising that both Rosset and Camus sometimes appear to implicate a vague, irrational and capricious force, which enjoys wreaking havoc on men's lives. Did vestiges of Rosset's previous Protestant convictions prompt the exclamation: 'O décrets de la fatalité, qui pourra sonder la profondeur de vos abimes! Nos jours sont comptés dès l'Eternité, et c'est en vain de vouloir prévenir ce qui doit arriver'? (*HM* II, p. 83). A more likely explanation lies in the syncretist tendencies of the age, which blended Christian and classical moral doctrines without always considering the difficulties inherent in so doing. This influence had been steadily increasing since Henri IV sanctioned the reopening of Jesuit colleges in 1603 and placed the philosophy of ancient Greece and Rome at the heart of education. As Sturel points out, an author referring to a moral lesson from Antiquity 'se fait épicurien avec Horace ou licencieux avec Anacréon, sans renoncer pour cela à ses croyances chrétiennes et à une morale toute différente'.[34] Rosset recognizes the incomprehension of believers when faced with seemingly senseless and cruel events and gives voice to their bewilderment, aware of their need to find some explanation for the horrors and uncertainties which had beset the turn of the century – the Wars of Religion, the assassination of Henri IV, the outbreaks of plague. Therefore, despite the pagan connotations of Rosset's 'dieux, apaisés par les larmes et par les cris des gens de bien' (*HM* II, p. 77) it is hard to justify Knutson's reference to 'the neo-pagan corpus' of Rosset's writing.[35]

It is more difficult to defend allusions made by a bishop to an ambiguous, often malicious, force that can take control of men's lives – particularly those made quite soon after the question of free will had been hotly debated by Mersenne and Garasse.[36] In one story, Camus speaks of 'cette persecution continuelle que la fortune enuieuse faict à la vertu', striking men down when they are in sight of their goal,[37] although, at other times, he maintains that man is entirely free from any such influence or feels obliged to clarify his position and reconcile his use of such terms with his Christian beliefs:

> Quand i'vse de ce mot de fortune, et icy et ailleurs, ie croy que le Lecteur fauorable ne m'estime pas si peu Chrestien, que ie le prenne à la mode des Anciens, qui n'estoient pas éclairez de la lumiere de iustice: mais par ce terme i'exprime les secrets ressorts de ceste Prouidence adorable.[38]

It would appear that when Camus uses the words *fortune* or *destin*, he does so not with any intention of contravening Catholic dogma but simply to indicate a train of events, either propitious or disastrous, which God permits for a purpose known only to Himself. For Camus, man is free in as much as his ultimate destiny – his salvation or damnation – is determined by his own choice. No power of Satan can force him to join with evil against his will if he calls upon and trusts in

God's help. Therein lies the '*libre arbitre*', the opportunity of salvation open to all, as opposed to Calvinist predestination, according to which a man's salvation or damnation was entirely predetermined by God and not susceptible to any mortal effort. Even so, he shows that his own acceptance of Providence's decrees can sometimes be sorely tested; having told the story of an industrious and virtuous young man, who died just before his wedding, he asks the reader: 'A vostre auis cet Inconnu si Reconnoissant ne meritoit il pas vne plus longue destinée?'.[39]

Vaucher de Gravili and Poli argue that the *histoires tragiques* largely follow the formula 'loi, transgression, punition', thereby implying that they demonstrate that the outcome of men's actions can be explained in a logical way.[40] However, the message the *histoire tragique* puts across very forcibly is that life is uncertain and that it is often very hard to find a logical explanation for good or bad fortune. Indeed, one of Rosset's stories shows how, ultimately, even a good deed can have tragic consequences. Jean Vaumorin, a former tailor, is rescued from a galley, to which he was sent after being involved in a robbery, thanks to the laudable intervention of his son, but he is too old to resume his trade successfully and resorts to crime, which leads to his execution.[41] In the *histoire tragique* the relationship between culpability and punishment is inconsistent, sin is not a prerequisite for a tragic outcome and complexities of the plot often make the attribution of guilt difficult. Furthermore, the formula 'law, transgression, punition' implies that there is one law only against which guilt is judged, whereas, as has already been demonstrated, in Camus's stories someone who appears innocent in the eyes of man may be deemed culpable by God.

Readers' attitudes towards the histoires tragiques

Whether the readers bought the stories with a view to moral improvement is certainly debatable. There was indeed much interest in the redemption of the soul and the afterlife; one third of books printed in Paris between 1598 and 1643 dealt with religious subjects,[42] and many works on purgatory appeared between 1580 and 1640.[43] Delumeau maintains that France, particularly at the time of the Catholic Reformation, was gripped by a collective guilt neurosis, 'une angoisse pathologique devant le jugement de Dieu, une surenchère de scruples, une rumination mentale du péché (originel, mortel et véniel), une fixation sur la mort'.[44] However, Céard believes that, even by the end of the sixteenth century, attitudes towards *histoires prodigieuses*, which, like the *histoires tragiques*, proclaimed a moralizing purpose, had undergone a marked change: 'Le temps n'était plus semble-t-il, à la crainte et à la méditation; une curiosité, qui ne dédaignait pas le piquant d'un peu d'inquiétude, voilà sans doute le sentiment qui animait le commun des lecteurs'.[45] In the Preface to *Les Evenemens singuliers* Camus himself laments, 'Mais las! Plusieurs lisent les liures par curiosité, d'autres par diuertissement, et au defaut de quelqu'autre entretien, d'autres par vanité, d'autres auec malignité, peu auec sincerité, peu auec desir de faire leur profit, et de mettre en pratique les enseignemens qu'ils y trouuent'. The public nevertheless retained its predilection for stories involving extraordinary, even bizarre, events, that illustrated the cruel suffering caused by man, pitiless Fortune, or a wrathful God, until the increasing importance given to *bienséance* put an end to ghoulish descriptions, and a refinement in tastes caused the popularity of the *histoire tragique* to decline in favour of a growing interest in the psychological aspects of characters' actions.

NOTES

[1] Erica Harth, *Ideology and Culture in Seventeenth-Century France* (Cornell University Press, 1983), p. 129.
[2] See Julia Horn's contribution to this volume, pp. 31-42.
[3] See, for example, Pierre Boaistuau, *Histoires prodigieuses* (1566).
[4] Jean-Pierre Camus, *L'Amphithéâtre sanglant,* ed. by Stéphan Ferrari (Champion, 2001), 'L'Auteur au lecteur', p. 179.
[5] Maurice Lever, *Canards sanglants: naissance du fait divers* (Fayard, 1993), p. 30.
[6] François de Rosset, *Les Histoires memorables et tragiques de ce temps, où sont contenues les morts funestes et lamentables de plusieurs personnes arrivees par leurs ambitions, amours desreiglees, sortileges, vols, rapines et par autres accidens divers,* ed. by Anne de Vaucher Gravili (Le Livre de Poche, 1994, based on Pierre Chevalier's 1619 edition), Histoire XVI, p. 359.
[7] Milton Bush Knutson, '(Dis)simulation and *tromperie* in the works of François de Rosset', doctoral thesis (University of Arizona, 1993), pp. 160 and 161.
[8] Pierre Charron, *De la Sagesse* (Fayard, 1986), Livre I, ch. 18, p. 157.
[9] *L'Amphithéâtre sanglant*, p. 180.
[10] Jean-Pierre Camus, *Les Diversitez* (M. Wyon, 1620), Tome IV, Livre 14, ch. viii, p. 55.
[11] Jean-Pierre Camus, *Les Rencontres funestes ou fortunes infortunées de nostre temps* (Jacques Villery, 1644), XLI, pp. 219-220.
[12] For example, Jean-Pierre Camus, *Les Spectacles d'horreur, où se descouvrent plusieurs effects de nostre siecle* (Slatkine Reprints, 1973), facsimile reprint of the first edition (A.

Saubron,1630), Livre I, 3 and 23, and Livre II, 13 and 14; *L'Amphithéâtre sanglant*, Livre II, 5 and 16, *Les Rencontres funestes*, 1 and 16.

[13] See Thierry Pech, 'Foy et secret: le mariage clandestin entre droit et littérature dans les Histoires tragiques de Boaistuau à Camus, *XVIIᵉ siècle*, oct.-déc., 1996, pp. 892-893.

[14] Wendy Gibson, *Women in 17th Century France* (Macmillan, 1989), p. 50.

[15] Thomas DiPiero, *Dangerous Truths and Criminal Passions, the Evolution of the French Novel, 1569-1791* (Stanford University Press, 1992), p. 32.

[16] *Les Spectacles d'horreur*, p. 246.

[17] *Les Histoires memorables*, XIX, p. 403.

[18] *L'Amphithéâtre sanglant*, II, 3, p. 294.

[19] See Michel de Montaigne, *Les Essais*, ed. by Jean Céard and others (Livre de Poche, 2001), Livre II, ch. 3, p.579.

[20] *Les Spectacles d'horreur*, I, 23, p. 258.

[21] *L'Amphithéâtre sanglant*, I, 3, p. 198

[22] *Ibid.*

[23] *Les Histoires memorables*, VIII, p. 232.

[24] *De la Sagesse*, Livre I, ch. 29, p. 191.

[25] *De la Sagesse*, Livre III, ch. 34, p. 775.

[26] Jean-Pierre Camus, *Les Succez différens* (Joseph Cottereau, 1630), I, 5, pp. 55-56.

[27] *Les Succez différens*, II, 9, p. 424.

[28] Jean-Pierre Camus, *Les Evenemens singuliers* (Jacques Cotinet, 1660), I, 9, p 204.

[29] *Les Spectacles d'horreur*, I, 4.

[30] *Les Spectacles d'horreur*, I, 9, p. 108

[31] Sergio Poli, *Storia di Storie: Considerazioni sull'evoluzione della storia tragica in Francia dalla fine delle guerre civili alla morte di Luigi XIII* (Piovan, 1985), p. 236, footnote 392: 'un degno personaggio'. Vanini contended that the world was eternal and that the motive cause of all action originates in an unspecified 'Providence' or in the stars, which not only guide but control man's will. See Edward J. Kearns, *Ideas in seventeenth-century France: the most important thinkers and the climate of ideas in which they worked* (Manchester University Press, 1979).

[32] *Storia di Storie*, p. 236, footnote 392: 'il tribunale, che avrebbe – secondo Rosset – voluto salvarlo, si vede invece praticamente costretto a condannarlo'.

[33] See Didier Foucault's reproduction of the text of *Les Histoires memorables*, V, with indications of Rosset's additions: http://lancelot.univ-paris12.fr/lc4-2c.htm.

[34] René Sturel, *Bandello en France au XVIᵉ siècle*, extrait du *Bulletin italien* (Annales de la Faculté des lettres de Bordeaux), t. 13-18 (Feret, 1918), p. 99.

[35] '(Dis)simulation and *tromperie* ...', p. 78.

[36] Marin Mersenne, *Impiété des déistes, et des libertins decouverte, et refutée* (1624); François Garasse, *La doctrine curieuse des beaux esprits de ce temps, ou pretendus tels* (1624).

[37] *Les Spectacles d'horreur*, I, 3, p. 29.

[38] *Les Evenemens singuliers*, II, 15, p. 387.

[39] Jean-Pierre Camus, *Les Leçons exemplaires* (Robert Bertault,1632), III, 7, p. 435.

[40] Anne de Vaucher Gravili, *Loi et Transgression: les histoires tragiques au XVIIᵉ siècle* (Milella, 1982); Sergio Poli, *Storia di Storie*.

[41] *Les Histoires memorables*, XII.

[42] Henri-Jean Martin, *Livre, pouvoirs et société à Paris au XVIIe siècle* (1598-1701) (Droz, 1969), p. 153.

[43] Michel Vovelle, *La Mort et l'Occident* (Gallimard, 1983), p. 308.

[44] Jean Delumeau, *Le péché et la peur: la culpabilisation en Occident* (Fayard, 1983), pp. 332-333.

[45] Jean Céard, *La Nature et les Prodiges: l'insolite au XVF siècle en France* (Droz, 1977), p. 479.

L'Interdit et ses limites dans
Erotika Biblion de Mirabeau

Isabelle Dotan-Robinet
Haifa University, Israel

En matière de moeurs, malgré les nombreux interdits encore bien présents dans les lois de la société française, le 18ᵉ siècle évolue en général vers une plus grande liberté qui se concrétise avec la Révolution de 1789. On s'étonne pourtant encore de certaines législations et de leur incongruité : on supprime par exemple la peine de mort pour sorcellerie (1731) mais on condamne les francs-maçons (1737) ainsi que tous ceux qui impriment, vendent ou diffusent des ouvrages tendant à troubler l'ordre (1757). Ceux-ci sont condamnés encore plus sérieusement que leur auteur[1]. Ce n'est qu'en 1787 qu'on abolit la corvée, la torture (1788) et la censure sur les écrits (1789), censure qui sera rétablie par le Conseil des Cinq-Cents en 1795. En matière de publication, les textes prohibés sont principalement ceux qui se rattachent au mouvement libertin en plein épanouissement à cette époque. Les premiers libertins[2] séparaient religion et morale ainsi que libertinage d'esprit et libertinage des moeurs pour dénoncer la corruption du milieu ecclésiastique alors que des agnostiques pouvaient montrer une vertu exemplaire. Ils réclamaient la liberté de conscience et même celle d'être athée. Les libertins, dont la plupart étaient matérialistes, pensent que l'âme dépend essentiellement des organes du corps avec lesquels elle se forme, croît et décroît. Le point de référence est la nature. La morale commune ressortissant de cette position est de faire ce qu'elle dicte puisqu'elle est bonne et parfaite. L'homme réintègre la nature et la matière qui encouragent l'épanouissement des instincts, la libération des sens en prenant, entre autres, exemple sur les animaux. Les problèmes surviennent lorsque l'on considère que cette nature, acceptée comme le modèle du comportement humain, doit maintenir une certaine morale afin de permettre une vie sociale raisonnable. Pour ce faire, les libertins introduisent alors deux critères supplémentaires : le plaisir et la raison. La Mettrie (1748) prétend que c'est de l'art de jouir que se développent tous les plaisirs et qu'au-delà du plaisir se trouve la volupté. De plus, le plaisir n'est pas exclusivement physique : 'Pas de jouissance de l'âme sans jouissance du corps'[3]. Cependant, il ne traite pas du problème social qui en résulte car l'excès de plaisir peut mener à la débauche et c'est plus spécifiquement sur ce point que la délimitation des interdits devient ardue. Les philosophes se penchent principalement sur le concept de 'raison' comme critère principal de délimitation. La raison est définie comme la norme absolue de la pensée humaine et est encore identifiée avec Dieu mais un Dieu différent de celui des institutions religieuses : 'La raison que nous consultons est une raison universelle (…) une raison immuable et nécessaire (…) ; s'il est vrai qu'elle est immuable et nécessaire, elle n'est pas différente de celle de Dieu.'[4]

Dans le contexte ici posé, il convient de distinguer d'une part la théorie qui est la réflexion de base des Matérialistes du 18ᵉ siècle et d'autre part la pratique qui est pensée et vécue par les libertins. Cette dernière position est fortement ressenti dans les romans libertins: derrière une intrigue érotico-pornographique, se dessine une réflexion philosophique qui critique souvent les Autorités. Les Œuvres Erotiques de Mirabeau[5] confirment cette double orientation : d'une part, le brillant philosophe matérialiste et d'autre part le libertin aux moeurs dépravées.

A l'encontre des romans érotico-pornographiques rassemblés dans Les Œuvres Érotiques de Mirabeau[6], Erotika Biblion est un essai. C'est dans le donjon de Vincennes, emprisonné par lettres de cachet par l'intervention de son propre père que Mirabeau l'écrit en quelques jours. L'édition originale fut publiée sous le manteau en 1783 et condamnée à la destruction par la Cour Royale de Paris à deux reprises (1783 et 1826).

Dans la forme, on y découvre un rebelle bafouant les interdits fixés par les Autorités en matière d'expression et de publication. Ensuite, dans le contenu, on retrouve les grandes idées des Matérialistes ainsi qu'un tempérament profondément libertin, une recherche presque excessive du plaisir des sens.

Le procédé de l'utopie

Le texte de base sur lequel Mirabeau se fonde pour faire le plaidoyer de ses idées est le texte le plus sacré de la civilisation judéo-chrétienne : la Bible. Avec audace et ironie, il publie Erotika Biblion 'A Rome, De l'Imprimerie du Vatican'. Il nargue ainsi l'autorité religieuse et politique en matière de censure et pour parfaire l'affront, il choisit un titre provocateur en confrontant deux mots incompatibles dans l'esprit judéo-chrétien ; Il est intéressant de remarquer qu'il ait choisi 'biblion' (livre) et non 'biblia' (livres saints). Il semblerait qu'il ait désiré garder dans le titre une certaine ambiguïté en laissant le choix de deux interprétations possibles : 'Livre d'érotisme' ou 'Erotisme dans la Bible' car même s'il est camouflé, le terme 'Biblion' implique certainement une référence à la Bible puisque Mirabeau y fait constamment allusion[7]. En jouant au théologien, il emploie des mots hébreux et grecs pour les titres du livre et des chapitres, reflétant ainsi sa volonté d'impressionner par des mots savants. Par son soit-disant savoir, il défie les Autorités. On peut se demander s'il s'agit là d'un simulacre ou d'une grande érudition mise à profit d'une fiction. Il est très probable que Mirabeau avait une Bible dans sa cellule (C'est souvent le seul livre autorisé en prison) et qu'il a su en tirer profit. Cependant, pour pouvoir se défendre et critiquer les Autorités libre de toute contrainte, Mirabeau abrite la Bible dans une fiction utopique à outrance. Ainsi le premier chapitre d'*Erotika Biblion* présente au lecteur un manuscrit mozarabique[8] découvert lors de fouilles archéologiques et révélant les moeurs d'une société imaginaire, idéale et parfaite qui touche à la dérision. Cette société se rapproche à peine des aspirations philosophiques du 18ᵉ siècle. Elle ne peut donc même pas servir de modèle puisque les personnages qui y vivent n'ont pas les mêmes conditions de vie que les humains. Comme dans toute utopie, c'est pourtant un monde clos et rigide, sans libre arbitre et qui, ironiquement rappelle l'emprisonnement. En se basant sur ces textes sacrés sous le couvert de ce manuscrit utopique et par l'introduction de personnages à la fois réels et imaginaires[9], Mirabeau ne réfute pas pour autant la valeur historique et culturelle de la Bible. Il sait aussi que la morale judéo-chrétienne repose sur les textes sacrés ; il en fait donc une réinterprétation. En faisant de l'archéologie littéraire il extrait les critères ou les arguments d'autorité à partir desquels il pourra justifier certaines moeurs condamnées par les institutions. C'est un plaidoyer en faveur des moeurs de son temps mais aussi une remise en question des moeurs libertines. En effet, à propos de sa réflexion sur l'écriture d'*Erotika Biblion* il écrit à Sophie Monnier[10] : 'Croirais-tu que l'on pourrait faire dans la Bible et l'antiquité des recherches sur l'onanisme, la tribaderie, etc. enfin sur les matières scabreuses qu'aient traitées les casuistes, et rendrent tout cela lisible même au collet le plus monté ?'[11]. Dans cette question, on pressent une certaine appréhension par rapport à ses lecteurs libertins, un souci concernant le dépassement des interdits même en milieu libertin.

Le critère de 'raison'

Tout en critiquant une société jugée corrompue, Mirabeau ne la condamne pas pour autant mais considère le changement de cette société, son remodelage, en jugeant que ce n'est plus l'Eglise qui doit déterminer les interdits mais les critères de raison et de morale. Il s'agit d'une raison éclairée qui bannit les dogmes, les préjugés et les superstitions de son temps. Mirabeau rejette la notion de péché, ce qui l'amène à définir un code moral basé sur le slogan : 'Ne pas nuire'. L'Homme occupe la place principale et est le seul responsable de ses actes dans un cadre social déterminé. Il met à l'épreuve les moeurs des Anciens face à celles de son siècle en se référant aux règles dictées directement par Dieu dans la Bible[12]. Cette stratégie est intéressante si l'on considère la position des philosophes du 18ᵉ siècle qui refusent en général l'idée d'un Dieu rémunérateur et vengeur tel qu'Il est représenté dans la Bible :

> La plupart d'entre eux (philosophes) rejette l'idée même d'une divinité titulaire de la morale, quelle qu'elle soit : il faut impérativement substituer à la garantie refusée une garantie efficace et crédible. C'est un nouveau fondement principe qui permettra d'encourager les hommes à pratiquer la vertu et respecter la morale.[13]

Ainsi, au lieu de s'éloigner de la religion, Mirabeau s'en sert de façon ironiquement fondamentaliste pour reconsidérer les règles de conduites humaines. Il extrait des arguments de la Bible à son gré pour faire l'apologie de ses propres idées Il donne aux lecteurs une interprétation personnelle de la parole divine et démystifie la Bible. Il s'en prend aussi aux théologiens : 'Voilà ce que nos théologiens, ignorants et vains, devraient nous apprendre. Le grand art est de lier toujours la science de la nature avec celle de la théologie, et non de faire heurter sans cesse des choses saintes et la raison, les croyants fidèles et les philosophes.'[14]

En faisant un exposé détaillé des moeurs sexuelles connues chez les Hébreux[15], Mirabeau use d'un raisonnement logique et arrive à justifier la pratique de certaines moeurs interdites de son temps. Sa tactique est de comparer les moeurs bibliques à celles du 18ᵉ siècle et de démontrer à quel point elles étaient et sont encore honorables. Par exemple, en démontrant comment Jésus est né de la descendance d'une série de femmes aux moeurs douteuses et interdites par la loi biblique (Ruth qui était non juive, Raab, une courtisane, Bethsabée, une prostituée et Tamar une incestueuse) il justifie les chemins de Dieu et adopte la plupart de ces coutumes pour son époque. Il fait allusion aux diverses pratiques de fornication, d'inceste, de pédophilie, d'onanisme, de polygamie, de bestialité qui sont mentionnées dans la Bible. Si on vérifie le texte original,[16] on se rend compte que Mirabeau le manipule car si les interdictions sont en effet énoncées dans la Bible cela ne veut pas dire que ces moeurs étaient pratiquées en toute liberté par les Hébreux ni qu'elles faisaient partie de leur vie quotidienne. Mais cela lui convient et ainsi de conclure : 'Encore une fois, nos coutumes sont-elles moins décentes que celles-là ? Et pourquoi exagérer nos torts et nos faiblesses [...] Ne vaut-il pas mieux tout adoucir, tout concilier ?'[17]

Mirabeau se sert du même critère de raison pour parler du statut de la femme[18]. Il puise dans l'histoire pour illustrer la disposition des femmes à la réflexion et la place qui leur revient dans la société. En remontant de Sapho à Marie Schurmann[19], il se veut admirateur des femmes et même féministe. Cependant, en biais on devine une position plus machiste qui redonne à la femme sa place d'objet sexuel aux yeux des hommes ; cela par diverses allusions rappelant constamment l'importance de sa beauté, de sa sensualité et sa disposition à l'amour. Par exemple même en parlant du culte de la Vierge il précise ironiquement qu'il s'agit d'un culte bien plus humain que celui de Dieu puisqu'il s'agit malgré tout d'une femme en chair et en os: '(...) le culte de la Vierge est bien plus approprié à l'esprit humain que celui du grand Être aussi inexplicable qu'incompréhensible.'[20] Et encore par rapport à Jésus, homme comme tous les autres ayant ses faiblesses envers les femmes : 'Enfin, le Sauveur a toujours eu pour les femmes une prédilection bien honorable à leur sexe.'[21]. L'ironie qui ressort de ces citations illustre bien le caractère burlesque d'*Erotika Biblion* et place Mirabeau dans la lignée des grands panégyristes.[22]

Le critère de "nature"

Cette orientation sexiste propre à Mirabeau est d'autant plus ressentie lorsqu'il se sert des critères de nature afin de mieux cerner les limites des interdits. Nous verrons plus tard qu'il en est de même pour le critère de plaisir. Cela pour dire que son féminisme est le résultat d'un raisonnement lucide et logique mais, apparemment, lorsqu'il s'agit de pratique, les bonnes résolutions s'estompent.

Rappelons que dans la pensée des philosophes du 18ᵉ siècle, la nature idéalisée est bonne et parfaite et représente le modèle du comportement humain dans le respect de l'autre. Ainsi, Mirabeau définit un principe de base 'Le principe général et peut-être unique de morale [...] : mal est ce qui nuit'[23] et pour déterminer ce qui nuit, il propose l'observation de la nature : 'C'est ainsi que dans toutes les opérations de la nature la beauté naît d'un ordre qui tend au loin, et qu'en voulant faire ce qui est bon elle a fait nécessairement en même temps ce qui lui plait.'[24] Par le biais de l'argument 'nature' il prouve aussi la légitimité de l'homosexualité et du lesbianisme. C'est encore avec beaucoup d'ironie qu'il interprète l'androgynat originel d'Adam comme l'origine de l'attraction de l'homme pour l'homme et prouve l'ancienneté et la légitimité de l'homosexualité qui est même présentée comme une erreur de Dieu[25] faisant partie intégrante de la nature. Pour mieux confirmer ses hypothèses, il se sert d'un texte de Platon qui confirme lui aussi cette théorie. Sur un ton railleur et simpliste il dit :

> C'est qu'il y avait trois sortes d'êtres dans le premier âge du monde : les uns mâles, les autres femelles, d'autres mâles et femelles tout ensemble ; [...] Dieu fit un miracle : il sépara les sexes [...] Il est arrivé de là et rien n'est plus simple, que le sexe femelle, séparé du sexe mâle, a conservé un amour ardent pour les hommes et que le sexe mâle aspire sans cesse à retrouver sa tendre et belle moitié. Mais il est des femmes qui aiment d'autres femmes ; rien de plus naturel encore : ce sont des moitiés de ces anciennes femelles qui étaient doubles. De mêmes certains males, dédoublements d'autres mâles, ont conservé un goût exclusif pour leur sexe.[26]

Il termine sa réflexion par un appel à la tolérance : 'Voyez combien quelques connaissances de plus ou de moins doivent donner plus ou moins de tolérance ! Je souhaite que ces idées en imposent aux moralistes déclamateurs. On peut leur citer des autorités graves car ce système, dont la source est dans Moïse, a été très étendu par le sublime Platon.'[27]

Le critère de 'plaisir'

Le dernier critère à examiner est celui de plaisir, car de l'observation de la nature on apprend que celle-ci agit par plaisir. Nous pensons que ce critère est de toute importance dans la détermination des limites des interdits ; cela, même si Mirabeau ne l'a pas utilisé de façon pertinente dans son analyse tel qu'il l'a fait avec les critères de 'raison' et 'nature'. Nous verrons que c'est d'ailleurs sur celui-ci que la délimitation des interdits selon Mirabeau se complique. Dans la pensée libertine, la notion de bonheur et de recherche du plaisir tient une place importante. Mirabeau y fait souvent allusion par un emportement des sens qu'on retrouve dans certaines descriptions détaillées du plaisir sexuel et qui rappelle ses romans érotiques.

C'est encore par l'intermédiaire du critère de raison qu'il accède à la notion de plaisir et qu'il démontre que les bienfaits du sexe ne nuisent ni au corps ni à l'esprit ; au contraire, le plaisir physique pourvoit au plaisir de l'âme : 'Mais quelle influence n'a-t-il pas sur toutes les parties de l'être ! Si le plaisir y existe, l'âme sensitive, agréablement émue, semble vouloir s'étendre, s'épanouir pour présenter plus de surface aux perceptions.'[28] Nous retrouvons ici les traits typiques du libertinage du 18ᵉ siècle. Par un raisonnement logique mais souvent manipulé, il défend ainsi l'onanisme[29] interdit dans la Bible, et encore au 18ᵉ siècle, mais ne nuisant à personne. Il répond ainsi au Docteur Tissot[30] qui, dans sa recherche sur l'onanisme prétendait qu'il ne s'agissait pas d'un péché contre Dieu mais contre la nature car 'les masturbateurs soustraient à la nature ce qui lui est nécessaire, et ce dont, par là-même, elle se gardait bien de se défaire'[31]. Tissot parle ainsi de cette terrible maladie qui déstabilise la société : 'les jeunes gens se dévirilisent, ils deviennent pâles, efféminés, engourdis, paresseux, lâches, stupides, et même imbéciles. Quand aux jeunes filles, certaines ne se contentent pas de la masturbation et deviennent tribades, s'emparant ainsi des fonctions viriles'[32] C'est avec beaucoup de complaisance que Mirabeau bafoue ces données soit-disant scientifiques relevant de la nature et reconnaît que 'la morale est toujours faible contre la passion'[33]. Et, par rapport aux commandements bibliques, il soutient que même si ceux-ci sont sacrés, Dieu est indulgent, ouvert et tolérant et donc les Autorités devraient faire de même.

La problématique du critère de 'plaisir' et l'inconstance d'Erotika Biblion

Il nous semble que le critère de plaisir pose un problème car il contredit souvent les critères précédents de raison et de nature. En effet, en matière de moeurs sexuelles, on peut trouver du plaisir en nuisant à autrui ou en se comportant contre nature (bestialité). Quelles sont alors les limites du plaisir ? Celui-ci semble souvent passer au-delà de tout autre argument. Il est étonnant, que l'auteur d' *Erotika Biblion* ne parle pas de certains interdits comme le viol, l'inceste, la pédophilie et le sadisme. Il se contente de rappeler que ces moeurs étaient courantes dans la Bible mais ne prend pas position par rapport à leur légitimité au 18e siècle. Cela laisserait-il à penser qu'elles seraient tolérables ? Cette lacune est ressentie par le lecteur que nous sommes comme une bévue dans *Erotika Biblion*. Il nous semble que sur ces points Mirabeau fait passer le critère de 'plaisir' avant ceux de 'morale', 'nature' et 'raison'.

En matière de sexe, Mirabeau est sensible aux violences sexuelles faites aux hommes (eunuques, circoncision) ou aux faiblesses des hommes (pâtres)[34] mais ne fait jamais allusion aux violences sexuelles faites aux femmes, ni aux enfants (pédophilie). Le seul point important relevé au sujet de la femme est son plaisir sexuel. Celui-ci est très souvent décrit avec précision dans les romans érotiques de Mirabeau[35].

Autre contradiction dans *Erotika Biblion* : pour légitimer la sodomie, Mirabeau détourne l'argument de "nature". Avec '*L'anelytroïde*', c'est-à-dire 'la femme privée de vulve', il se penche sur la question des 'jouissances contre notre nature actuelle'. La question est si 'an imperforata mulier possit concipere[36] ?' et Mirabeau passant pour un faux naïf dit : 'C'est que beaucoup de jeunes femmes stériles sont autorisées, et doivent même en conscience tenter les deux voies, jusqu'à ce qu'elles se soient assurées de la véritable route que le Créateur a mise en elles.'[37] Les diverses tactiques moqueuses, ironiques et satiriques utilisées par Mirabeau pour prouver ses arguments déroutent parfois le lecteur mais donne à *Erotika Biblion* un aspect burlesque, dirions-nous même mirabesque !

Le monde utopique dans lequel s'ouvrait *Erotika Biblion* présentait une société où l'homme vit dans un bonheur total où ses besoins étaient toujours satisfaits dans le cadre de limites claires et nettes posées par une nature parfaite et harmonieuse. En fait, il n'y a pas d'interdit puisque tout est limité d'avance dans un monde parfait. On devine rapidement que ce n'est pas l'idéal poursuivi par Mirabeau car si l'homme n'a pas de libre arbitre, que reste-t-il de sa créativité, de sa liberté de choix. C'est là peut-être que l'on touche à l'humanisme de Mirabeau. Petit à petit, l'utopisme fait place à une réalité proche des lecteurs du 18e siècle. A l'opposé de ce monde utopique, il propose l'homme avec ses qualités et ses défauts, l'homme se battant pour sa liberté, l'homme éclairé critiquant le pouvoir politique et religieux qui use de la peur afin de faire respecter les lois des moeurs et tend des pièges afin de colleter les réfractaires. Ce qu'il critique avant tout ce sont ces lois qui déterminent les interdits selon des règles superstitieuses qui manquent de sagesse et qui sont rédigées par des 'faiseurs de lois' qu'il traite 'd'étroitesse d'esprit et de mauvais cœurs' pour substituer la terreur au respect qu'ils ne peuvent obtenir.

Erotika Biblion se veut, avant tout, un inventaire des moeurs sexuelles que Mirabeau tente de classer selon des degrés d'admission en milieu déjà libertin. (On ne peut imaginer qu'il ait sérieusement pensé propager ses idées aux institutions de son temps). Il se montre partisan de l'amour libre et de nombreuses pratiques sexuelles souvent interdites par l'Eglise (l'onanisme, la masturbation, la sodomie, la fellation, le droit au plaisir sexuel pour la femme, l'homosexualité, le lesbianisme, l'inceste). Par contre, il condamne d'autres moeurs comme la castration, la circoncision et la bestialité.

Il va sans dire qu'avec *Erotika Biblion* Mirabeau ouvre les portes à la liberté sexuelle. Il le fait avec ironie et humour, ce qui donne au texte un caractère burlesque et confirme la volonté de Mirabeau de défier les Autorités par la dérision. On ne peut cependant ignorer le coté philosophique de cet essai où l'on retrouve les idées matérialistes des libertins du 18e siècle dont le principe de base est le plaisir.

NOTES

[1] Concernant la publication de Erotika Biblion : on arrête François Mallet, libraire à Neuchâtel, le 30 juin 1783 dont on sait qu'il a 'payé à monsieur le comte de Mirabeau la somme de 100 louis pour le manuscrit d'Erotika Biblion' - Jean Marie Goulemot, *Ces livres qu'on ne lit que d'une main*, (Alinea, 1991), p. 27.

[2] Voir Pierre Bayle (17e siècle) – *Petit Robert des Noms propres* (Robert, 1995), p. 209.

[3] De la Mettrie Julien Offray, *De la volupté*, (Desjonqueres, 1996).

[4] Nicolas Malebranche, *De la Recherche de la vérité*, (Vrin, 1675).

[5] Honoré Gabriel de Riquetti, comte de Mirabeau *Oeuvres érotiques de Mirabeau*, L'Enfer de la Bibliothèque Nationale 1, (Librairie Arthème Fayard, 1984).

[6] *Ma conversion, Hic et Haec, Le rideau levé*, tous recueillis dans *Oeuvres érotiques de Mirabeau* – Ibid.

[7] Il est à noter que la Bible est une série de livres dont un est spécialement érotique (Le Cantique des Cantiques). Mirabeau se base pourtant principalement sur le Lévitique qui traite surtout des interdits sexuels.

[8] Du mot 'mozarabe' (chrétiens d'Espagne sous occupation arabe) mais peut-être aussi basé sur un jeu de mots : 'mosaïque' ?

[9] Ainsi cite-t-il Platon, Sanchez (jésuite espagnol ayant traité des questions du mariage et de la reproduction), Jésus, Moïse (et autres personnages bibliques) un certain Tauchelin (?), un scientifique M. Louis (?) le pape Benoît XIV (qui promut l'enseignement des sciences naturelles et scientifiques dans un sens très libéral), les Pères Cucuse (?) et Tournemine (jésuite), etc. Ses notes contiennent des références parfois véridiques, souvent douteuses : 1er chapitre, note 3 et 4 sont des références qui n'apparaissent pas dans le texte biblique : *Daniel XIV* et *I Maccabées* n'existent pas).

[10] Sophie Monnier, épouse du marquis de Monnier, avec qui Mirabeau s'était enfui en Suisse.

[11] Mirabeau, *Oeuvres érotiques*, p.449.

[12] Au dix-huitième siècle, l'église catholique se base principalement sur la Vulgate et les commentaires de la Bible. Pour son essai, Mirabeau se sert d'une approche plus fondamentaliste de la Bible car elle convient mieux à ses fins.

[13] Domenech Jacques, *L'Ethique des lumières ; les fondements de la morale dans la philosophie française du 18e siècle* (Librairie Philosophique J. Vrin , 1989, p. 72.

[14] Mirabeau, *Oeuvres érotiques*, p.477.

[15] Selon le 'Lévitique XII' dans Louis Segond, *La Bible* (Jongbloed Leeuwarden, 1910) et Mirabeau, *Oeuvres érotiques*, p. 500-501.

[16] Louis Segond, *La Bible* (Jongbloed Leeuwarden, 1910).

[17] Mirabeau, *Oeuvres érotiques*, p.503.

[18] Mirabeau, *Oeuvres érotiques* Chapitre 3, 'L'Ischa', p. 487.

[19] 'Anne-Marie de Schurmann, femme d'un savoir extraordinaire, née à Cologne en 1607' Commentaire de Mirabeau, Mirabeau, *Oeuvres érotiques*, p. 489.

[20] Mirabeau, *Oeuvres érotiques*, p.491.

[21] Mirabeau, *Oeuvres érotiques*, p. 492.

[22] Technique déjà connue avec *L'éloge de la folie* d'Erasme.

[23] Mirabeau, *Oeuvres érotiques*, p. 518.

[24] Mirabeau, *Oeuvres érotiques*, p.539.

[25] Mirabeau, *Oeuvres érotiques*, p.524.

[26] Mirabeau, *Oeuvres érotiques*, p. 524.

[27] Mirabeau, *Oeuvres érotiques*, p.523.

[28] Mirabeau, *Oeuvres érotiques*, p.541.

[29] 'Onanisme'/'masturbation chez l'homme' qui aboutit à la 'souillure sexuelle' (sperme perdu en vain) à différencier de 'masturbation' : "Pratique qui consiste à provoquer le plaisir sexuel par l'excitation manuelle des parties génitales du sujet ou du partenaire – *Petit Robert 1* 9Le Robert, 1990).

[30] M. Tissot-D.M, *L'onanisme, ou dissertation physique sur les maladies produites par la masturbation*, (A. Chapuis, 1760).

[31] Theodore Tarczylo, 'Représentations de la vie sexuelle' *Dix-huitième siècle* [Journal] Vol. 12, (Société française d'étude du XVIIIe siècle, 1980), p.85.

[32] Tarczylo, 'Vie sexuelle', *Dix-huitième siècle*, Ibid., p. 89.

[33] Mirabeau, *Oeuvres érotiques* p. 515.

[34] Dans les deux chapitres '*Kadesch*' et '*Behemah*', Mirabeau s'indigne de certaines pratiques sexuelles comme la castration considérée comme nuisance, et la bestialité considérée 'contre-nature'. Il manifeste encore une certaine inconstance lorsqu'il exprime son mépris envers les 'femmes juives' qui dans la Bible pratique la bestialité mais se montre indulgent envers les 'pâtres des Pyrénées' qui la pratiquent par besoin puisque l'éloignement de la société justifie l'acte.

[35] Ma conversion, Hic-et-haec et Le rideau levé in Mirabeau, *Oeuvres érotiques*

[36] Une fille 'imperforée' peut-elle concevoir ?

[37] Mirabeau, *Oeuvres érotiques*, p. 182.

Die Another Day: *Amadis de Gaule* and the Absence of Heroic Death[1]

Julia Horn
University of Cambridge

Amadis de Gaule, the twenty-one volume prose romance which had great success in mid-sixteenth-century France, poses an interesting problem to a volume devoted to the subject of the forbidden.[2] Very little is forbidden to the heroes and heroines of this multi-authored romance; indeed, it became known in part because of the scandalous nature of some of its content. Critics blamed it for inspiring the lax behaviour of young women in the period, and for the alarming rise in duelling and wanton violence among young men.[3] In the various narratives of the series, the knights defeat giants, monsters and pagans in war and in jousts. They run off with young princesses, tempting them into bed and allowing the narrator to indulge in sex scenes. They deal with the forces of magic as well as of evil; they are learned and chivalric, virtuous and full of lust, yet in spite of their illicit love affairs and clandestine marriages they usually become kings or emperors.[4]

However, neither the eponymous Amadis de Gaule, nor any of his male descendants will die, either in battle or through old age. Death is not totally absent from the series: the princesses may die in childbirth or in miscarriage (although some will live eternally alongside their heroic husbands) and the enemies of the knights will frequently die in battle against the protagonists of the series. Even troops on the side of Amadis and his descendants will die: in Book 10, for example, the battlefield becomes a sea of blood through the wholesale slaughter of troops on both sides. But Amadis and his direct male descendants do not die until the series itself finishes with Book 21 (1581). In a study of *Amadis*, John J. O'Connor concluded that 'in short, all the fighting, blood and violence of *Amadis* seems to hurt only the wicked',[5] but his summary does not describe with sufficient accuracy the way in which only a specific group of characters are immune. In *Amadis*, it is only the status of being a knight who is both a descendant of Amadis de Gaule and at some stage at the foreground of the narrative, which grants immunity to death.

There is a curious history to the untouchable status of the
Amadisian hero. In the original Spanish series, Paez de Ribera published
a continuation to Montalvo's five books in which Amadis de Gaule did
die. In Ribera's narrative, Oriane retired to a monastery upon the news of
her husband's death, and Galaor, the brother of Amadis, repented of his
ways and converted to become a monk. In Spain this new version of
Amadís was poorly received and was never reprinted. Thus, when this
section of the series was translated into French by Nicolas Herberay des
Essarts, Ribera's book was dropped from the series, and Amadis
remained alive. In the French series, however, there are several points in
the narrative at which alternative versions of the story (which always
involved the death of Amadis) are repudiated. For example, in Book 5,
the narrator denies an alternative narrative in which Esplandian kills his
father, Amadis, in a joust.

> Tout cela est faulx, et controuvé [...]. Et ne sçay penser ou telz,
> controuveurs de mensonges, leur ont inventé une si malheureuse
> fin, s'ilz ne veulent prendre pour mort les tenebres qu'Esplandian
> meit aux haults faitz de son pere, par la lumyere et illustration
> des siens. (52942: 5. 15, 29r)

Here, the potential loss of heroic status is conceived of as a metaphorical
death. The 'false' stories of Amadis's death threaten not only heroism,
but also the author's task of commemorating the hero. Thus belief in the
alternative and false narrative threatens not just heroism, but also the
writing process.

Book 8 will repeat the repudiation of alternative endings: 'aucuns
depuis ont fait autre le livre de Lisuart', states the narrator, 'ou ils font
mort le Roy Amadis: ce qui est clairement faus et faint, d'autant qu'il eût
vie longue deux cent ans et plus, et lors qu'ils le dient expiré, il n'en eut
peu avoir soisant' (53053: 8. 96, 181v).[6] Once more, the need to affirm
that Amadis did not die seems to gain greater significance than the simple
repudiation of alternative versions of *Amadis*. This second denial of death
even goes so far as to contravene verisimilitude and to suggest that, like a
biblical giant, Amadis was blessed with exceptional longevity. The
conception of heroism and of its commemoration in *Amadis* seems to
necessitate a fiction which makes Amadis into a super-human character.
Yet at the same time the narratives are haunted by this possibility of

Amadis dying. In keeping Amadis alive, this stretching of fictional boundaries serves to maintain the author's claim that he is telling a 'true' story: an apparent paradox which the series does not seek to resolve.

In *Amadis*, that which is forbidden – the death of the hero – thus reveals tensions inherent in chivalric romance and in the representation of heroism. The absence of death for the heroes in *Amadis* is more complex than just the simple omission of a narrative event which would seem logical to the modern reader. Instead, it invokes a series of conflicts or potential problems within the series, focused around heroic commemoration and literary production, around 'truth' and fiction, and around the representation of heroism.

Marketing *Amadis*

When posing the question of why Amadis does not die, the most obvious reason that presents itself to the modern scholar is the utility it provides the translators and publishers of the French series. In the original Spanish and Italian, only the first four books of the *Amadis* series bear the title of *Amadís de Gaula*. Continuations to the series were known by the names of their protagonists. For example, Book 5 was called *Sergas de Esplandian* (the deeds of Esplandian), Esplandian being the son of Amadis. In Book 5 (1544) of the French *Amadis*, however, Esplandian is relegated to a secondary position behind his father and the book is entitled '*Le Cinquiesme livre d'Amadis de Gaule, contenant partie des faitz chevalereux de Esplandian son filz et autres*'.[7] This convention is maintained in the whole of the French series. Book 20 (1581), for example, has the following title:

> *Le Vingtiesme et penultime livre d'Amadis de Gaule, Traittant des amours, gestes et faicts heroïques de plusieurs illustres et vertueux princes de la race et souche dudict Amadis.* (53092)

Even at this distance from the original narrative of Amadis, told in Books 1 to 4, the relationship to the original Amadis is emphasized at the cost of the names of these later protagonists. The result of this convention is to reunite under one name all twenty-one books, to emphasize their unity above their diversity and above all, to sell them to the public as a single series, with the implicit promise that each new book has the same ingredients which have previously pleased the reading public. This use of the single name represents a significant use of sales techniques in reaction to the high volumes of books the printing presses were able to produce.[8]

Reproducing *Amadis*

Of course, it is not essential that Amadis be kept alive in the narrative in order to market the later books of the series under the same title. It is the genealogical relationship to Amadis, and not his continuing presence in the series, which is emphasized in these title pages. It is tempting to assume that there must be an analogy between the longevity of the male protagonists of *Amadis* and the length of the series, and to see in the knight a textual representation of the continuation of the writing process. However, as each book or set of books focuses on a new generation of knights, the length of a lifetime is no barrier to the continuation of the series. It is procreation, not longevity, which prolongs the writing process, and the knights in *Amadis* are tremendously fertile. The production of suitable sons is never an issue.[9]

Nonetheless, the presence of Amadis throughout the series does have a unifying effect. For although his descendants do not die either, the remarks on longevity or on the lack of death tend to focus on Amadis. Thus, it is with the character Amadis that the absence of death becomes symbolic of a heroic status. The name, the value of heroism and the value of the series become intrinsically linked. Furthermore, although his descendants will be just as heroic, they will not be perfect characters. Amadis de Gaule is faithful in love, a good ruler, and an excellent knight. Amadis de Grece (Books 7 and 8) on the other hand, will not be faithful in love; Lisuart de Grece (Book 6) will have a hot temper, and will accidentally kill an innocent man. We could argue that the unparalleled virtue of Amadis de Gaule allows these descendants, as copies of the original, to differ from the model of perfection. Amadis thus stands not only as the original knight of the series, but also as the standard by which we measure all the others.[10] He gives the French series this thematic unity as well as the formal unity of the series title.

Amadis has influence on the series both through his continuing presence, and through his genealogical line. His reproductive influence is reinforced through specific episodes in the narrative. The first time Amadis returns to the narrative when he is no longer its protagonist (which is the case after the close of Book 4) is early in Book 5. Disguised in his armour, he challenges his own son, Esplandian, to fight:

> Et à dire vray, si Dieu n'y eust pourveu le pere eust mis à mort le filz, et le filz le pere. Car c'estoit Amadis lequel trop curieux de la gloire de son filz, le voulut esprouver. (5. 15, 28v)

This fight is so finely balanced that neither father nor son is able to win, the only possible outcome being that both participants should die from their wounds. Just in time, the battle is stopped and the son recognizes his father.[11] Afterwards, Amadis justifies his actions:

> J'avoye envyé qu'on cogneut la difference de noz deux forces, sçachant bien en tout avenement que le pis ne m'eust sçeu tourner qu'a louenge: car si mon filz me surpasse de quelquechose, sa gloire augmente la mienne passée. (5. 15, 29v)

In this brief episode the fight between Esplandian and Amadis represents a transmission of chivalric valour from father to son. The demonstration of the equivalence of their chivalric skills is not only a marker of family inheritance but also of innate nobility. This type of episode will reoccur. In Book 6, Amadis, Esplandian, Lisuart and Perion all fight, and afterwards the magician Alquif declares: 'il n'estoit pas raisonnable qu'aulcun de vous quatre eust l'honneur de ceste meslée: car vous n'estes qu'une mesme chose, une mesme chair, et (quand tout est dit) une mesme force et prouesse' (53048: 6. 28, 63r). In Book 8, a similar fight will take place between Lisuart and Amadis de Grece. These combats reinforce the ideology of chivalric romance, which depends upon a genealogical transmission of valour and nobility. This consanguinity is a reminder of another contemporary corpus of texts in which transmission from father to son is equally important: the four books of Rabelais. In a letter from Gargantua to his son, Pantagruel, the process of descent along the male line is described in similar terms. Gargantua describes fatherhood as a means to acquire immortality:

> L'humaine nature [...] peut, en estat mortel, acquerir une espece de immortalité, et en decours de vie transitoire, perpetuer son nom et sa semence. Ce qui est fait par lignée yssue de nous en

mariage legitime. Dont nous est aulcunement instauré ce qui nous a été tollu par le peché de noz premiers parents, esquels fut dit que, parce qu'ilz n'avoient esté obédiens au commandement de Dieu le createur, qu'ilz mourroient.[12]

For Gargantua, fatherhood does not actually make him immortal, only metaphorically so. However, it is curious that the Amadisian version of this regeneration is the literalization of this metaphor of self-perpetuation. As Gargantua emphasizes: 'quand [...] mon ame laissera ceste habitation humaine, je ne me reputeray point totallement mourir, mais plustost transmigrer d'ung lieu en aultre, attendu que, en toy et par toy, je demeure en mon ymage visible en ce monde' (Ch. 8, p. 86). At stake here again is the relationship between father and son, and the necessity of producing a male heir in order to retain the family estates. What is interesting is that Gargantua describes his death as a transformation, 'plustost transmigrer d'ung lieu en aultre'. The mortality of Gargantua is thus not conceived as an end but merely a change in form. The father will continue to haunt the son and to remain with him, even beyond death. Indeed, in *Pantagruel*, this curious metaphor will itself become literalized when, in Chapter 15, Pantagruel will learn that 'son pere avoit esté translaté au pays des Phées par Morgue, comme fut jadis Enoch et Helye'.[13] Marie-Madeleine Fragonard notes that 'la translation chez les fées est une forme de mort réservée aux héros. [...] Le rapprochement avec Énoch et Élie, emportés au ciel, mêle les prophètes bibliques aux fées du cycle arthurien'.[14] Thus once again biblical and romance motifs are mingled in the representation of a hero who will not die. The removal of Gargantua from the narrative acts only as a virtual death, which permits Pantagruel to combat the invading Dipsodes and so establish his own worth as a leader and king in his own right. The 'translation' of Gargantua permits the establishment of Pantagruel as a leader – a father figure – rather than as a son.[15] However, Gargantua's 'death' is not permanent, for he returns in the *Tiers Livre* in order to re-establish authority over his son in the matter of the preparations for his own marriage (and, by extension, fatherhood).

The relevance of these Rabelaisian fictions to *Amadis* and to the preservation of the male hero – which is, after all, quite different to that of Rabelais, in which the characters do not survive their descendants nor display exceptional heroism – is the manner in which Amadis disappears and reappears in the narratives. The model of a father who imposes his image upon his son and disappears in order to allow him to establish his own authority, but who may also reappear in order to influence events, is characteristic of *Amadis*. For in *Amadis* the hero is repeatedly enchanted or made younger, in order to allow him to both disappear from the plot and reappear at critical moments.

The first enchantment to remove Amadis from the narrative, along with his son Esplandian, in order that the children Lisuart and Perion many prosper, takes place at the end of Book 5. Urgande, a magician figure, explains why she wishes to enchant these knights:

> Tout ainsi que par la prescience et grand bonté du seigneur Dieu toutes choses ont esté establies: aussi luy a il pleu que toutes choses temporelles se passent et prennent fin par mort differente, selon la qualité de ce qu'il a crée. [...] Or sçay je pour certain, que la fin de voz ans est prochaine [...] Neanmoins premier que mort vous surpreigne, je vous veulx à tous monstrer l'amour que je vous ay portée, et feray tant avecq l'ayde de Dieu que (sans mourir) demourerez endormis, jusques au temps qu'un descendent de vous, vous delivrera de ce sommeil. (5. 56, 115v)

Here Urgande makes clear that the deferral of death permits both a removal of the older knight from the narrative, the promotion of a new hero ('un descendent de vous') and yet retains the possibility of a return to life. When released from this enchantment part way through Book 6, these characters will have been asleep for ten years. In Book 9, a similar enchantment will suspend the lives of the heroes for fifteen years, and in Book 10, the title of chapter 65 tells, in a Rabelaisian turn of phrase, 'comme le roy Amadis fut enlevee et transporté par les sages'. Enchantment also allows for a telescoping of timescales, allowing descending generations to co-exist and setting aside the problem of ageing. The removal and return of the 'father figure' thus allows the narrative to move forward, yet also to continually refer back to its origins.

Amadis and Technology

One of the characteristics of the episode in which Amadis returns is that he takes up the role of a chivalric and virtuous warrior, rather than that of a lover or a knight on an individual quest. We might say that this return is more closely linked to epic than to traditional romance themes. Indeed, the most common time at which Amadis returns to reassert his authority is in the event of a full-scale war. These wars, in which Christians defeat pagans, punctuate the narratives at regular intervals, notably in Books 5, 6, 10, 13, 19 and 21. In these battles, the role of Amadis is to be the best knight in the world, a phrase often used. In Book 10, the narrator uses this quality to explain the ability of Amadis to fight at an advanced age:

> Chacun s'esbahissoit, principallement du roy Amadis, auquel l'aage sembloit denyer telle verdeur: mais en luy estoit une vertu heroïque, qui ne tomboit en compariason de nul autre du monde, et ne se pouvoit encores amortir par le cours des ans. (52901: 10. 27, 59v)

The narrator here acknowledges the astonishment which the readers may well have felt at the longevity of Amadis. His comment reveals that the absence of death was feared to strain the credulity of readers. However, this same incredulity is placed in the mouths of the other characters in the diegesis, thus turning the heroism of Amadis into an extraordinary event even in the fictional world. The technique serves to once more turn a lack of verisimilitude into a marker of heroic qualities.

Indeed, *Amadis* seems to exploit rather than to avoid this link between heroism and incredible fiction. From relatively realistic battle scenes in the early books which tally closely with sixteenth-century historical evidence on warfare, the series moves towards ever more idealized battles. In Books 1 to 6, battle scenes are accompanied by detailed descriptions of the movements of the infantry, archers and even artillery who accompany the knights.[16] It is fascinating that *Amadis* does initially represent battle scenes which use new technologies such as gunpowder, when romance in this period is traditionally thought to eschew these developments. However, by Book 21 the battle scene has become unrealistically composed of knights on horseback alone:

> En ce temps là, toute la force des armes consistoit en la cavalerie, et ne se soucioyt l'on pas beaucoup de l'infanterie, que l'on menoit plustost pour la garde d'un camp [...] que pour combatre en compagne. (53903: 21. 116, 426v)

Idealization of the value of knighthood on the battlefield seems to increase in *Amadis* with the length of the series, the growing age of Amadis, and perhaps also the declining relevance of the knight to warfare in contemporary sixteenth-century society. Certain sixteenth-century critics questioned the purpose of the idealized and imaginary representation of chivalry in *Amadis*. François de La Noue, for example, remarked in the 1580s that 'quand un gentilhomme aurait toute sa vie leu les livres d'Amadis, il ne seroit ni bon soldat ne bon gendarme'.[17] Criticisms such as this one were certainly part of the reason why the popularity of *Amadis* declined as the century wore on.

Concluding Remarks: Death and Closure
Throughout this paper, I have explored the reasons why Amadis and his descendants do not die, but not his actual death at the end of the series. In the last two chapters of Book 21, the majority of the male heroes, including Amadis de Gaule, are killed in an epic battle between pagan and Christian forces. In this (rather sudden) conclusion to the series, which is announced from the title page of Book 21 but not enacted until the final six chapters,[18] the last battle is represented as a conclusive final struggle between the forces of good and evil:

> De part et autre estoit la fleur des Payens et des Chrestiens, pource qu'il sembloit que de la fin de ceste grande guerre, despendit l'entiere destruction, ou exaltation, de l'un ou l'autre empire. (21. 116, 427r)

However, even in this battle, the depiction of Amadis's death is characteristic of the concerns that previously prevented him from being defeated at all:

> Et durant le combat [...] deux geans occirent le grand et tres fameux Amadis de Gaule, fleur et miroir de toute la chevalerie du monde, en combattant vaillament, lequel en courtoisie et amour à l'endroit de sa belle et bien aymee dame la Roine Oriane, a donné exemple au monde, de fidelité à tous amans, et lequel en

liberalité, en justice, magnificence et grandeur de courage, a
surpassé tous les autres de son temps. (21. 121, 443r-444r)

In this passage, heroism is placed in the foreground and defeat is played
down in favour of the values that Amadis has always represented. A
narrative of the events of his life dominates and overshadows the scene of
death, which is quickly passed over at the beginning of the phrase, almost
as if it is unimportant. Thus, even at a local level and at the final moment
of death, the narrative repeats the technique of the series as a whole, and
death is once more elided and replaced with a narration of heroic acts.

Furthermore, due to the refusal of *Amadis* to depict a defeat of
chivalric values, Book 21 of *Amadis* fails to close the series with the
defeat of the Christian Empire. Instead, although the majority of the
heroes are killed, so are the pagan kings, and the few remaining
Christians are declared victors. The irony of this ending is that in
allowing the Christians to win the war and a few knights to survive the
wholesale round of deaths, the author of Book 21, so anxious to finish the
series, in fact leaves room for a continuation. This possibility will be
fulfilled in the French series with the publication in 1617 of three further
books of *Amadis*, nearly forty years after the 1581 publication of Book
21. It seems that narrative closure cannot be given to the series without
destroying the very values upon which this sixteenth-century chivalric
romance is based: *Amadis* is unable to lay to rest its heroes and to
imagine that death and valour can exist together. This strains the credulity
of readers but the conjoining values of chivalry, heroism and genealogy
make it impossible to negotiate a different outcome to the series, even
when the author's aim is closure. It is striking to see the extent to which
form and content are thus implicated together in a generic aesthetic of
chivalric romance.

These aspects of *Amadis* have a wider relevance to the
development of romance in France. In 1547, Jacques Amyot proposed an
alternative romance model: his own translation of the Greek romance of
Heliodorus, the *Histoire Æthiopique*. In a preface to the translation,
Amyot argues that the superiority of the Greek romance rests on certain
formal aspects. First, it is verisimilitudinous, that is to say, its fictions do
not exceed the bounds of the possible. Second, the narrative has a clear
structure with a beginning, a middle, and an end. However, for Amyot,
the *Histoire Æthiopique* lacks one important element: heroism. He writes:

ce n'est qu'une fable, à laquelle encore default (à mon jugement) l'une des deux perfections requises pour faire une chose belle, c'est la grandeur, à cause que les contes, mesmement quant à la personne de Theagenes, auquel il ne fait executer nulz memorables exploitz d'armes, ne me semblent point assez riches.[19]

The Greek romance renounces two of the formal aspects of *Amadis*, but it is unable to make these changes and maintain the heroism for which *Amadis* is famous. In this period, romance representations of heroism seem to preclude death or narrative closure.

NOTES

[1] The inspiration for this paper was the idea that *Amadis* has much in common with the James Bond series. Like James Bond, *Amadis* retained its popularity over a long period of time. In both the eponymous hero is notorious for his success with women, his heroism and his survival of dangerous situations. Above all, in both the hero upholds values that are arguably representative of a bygone era. James Bond is a British spy from the cold war, still able to evade death in an age in which American military technology has rendered redundant the notion of an individual hero. Amadis likewise upholds individualistic chivalric values that are becoming obsolete with the technology of gunpowder and the rise of the educated nobility (the *noblesse de robe*) at court.

[2] The twenty-one volumes of the French series of *Amadis* were published between 1540 and 1581, and were all translations from either Spanish or Italian. Although there is no modern publication of the series currently available, digitalized versions of the originals are available to download via the Gallica site: http://gallica.bnf.fr. The five-digit numerical references in this article, e.g. 52942, are Gallica document numbers, and the page references are expressed in the form of book number, chapter, and folio or page number, e.g. 1. 1, 1r.

[3] These criticisms mostly come after 1560, the series having initially been a great success. The most extended attack upon the series is that of François de la Noue, who devoted a chapter of his *Discours politiques et militaires* to *Amadis*.

[4] This mixture of both epic and romance qualities (empire-building and crusading as well as the individual quest and love story) is typical of many sixteenth-century romances, which are often thought of as a hybrid 'epic romance' genre.

[5] *Amadis de Gaule and its Influence on Elizabethan Literature* (Rutgers University Press, 1970). p. 41

[6] Some people since have made an alternative version of Lisuart's book, in which King Amadis is killed off. This is clearly false and faked, all the more so since he had a long

life of two hundred years or more, and when they say that he has died, he could not have been sixty.

[7] The fifth book of Amadis de Gaule, containing a part of the chivalrous deeds of Esplandian his son and others.

[8] On *Amadis* as a phenomenon success in terms of the printing press, see Stephen Rawles, 'The Earliest Editions of Nicolas de Herberay's Translations of *Amadis de Gaule' The Library* 8 (1981), 91-105 and Michel Simonin, 'Le disgrace d'Amadis' *Studi francesi* 28:1 (1984),1-35.

[9] This is in itself remarkable. Medieval romance often explores the anxieties behind the need for male issue in order to continue a household. Rabelais's texts also reveal anxieties with regard to procreation, notably in the *Tiers livre*, in which Panurge is unable to decide whether or not to marry. *Amadis* could therefore be seen as attempting to resolve the problem of male continuation through an idealization of the processes of mariage and procreation.

[10] It is also a standard by which they judge themselves. There are many scenes in which the knights compare their own valour to that of their forefathers, usually finding themselves wanting in comparison.

[11] Testing the equal prowess between blood relations is a romance convention. In the thirteenth-century *Perlesvaus* Lancelot fights his uncle Percival to similar effect.

[12] *Pantagruel*, ed. Marie-Madeleine Fragonard (Pocket, 1997), p. 84.

[13] *Pantagruel*, p. 216.

[14] *Pantagruel*, p. 216n.

[15] I owe the term 'father figure' to Carla Freccero, who interprets Gargantua's role here as that of an epic hero who becomes the 'absolute, simpler and more serene past to which the present protagonists cannot return'. When Gargantua reappears in the *Tiers livre*, Freccero argues that he stands in opposition to the pyrrhonist philosophy of Trouillogan: 'the nostalgia for a return to a less confusing, clearer past, when philosophers presumably could be "taken at their word" is nowhere more apparent, and joined to this nostalgia is also a nostalgia for a reunion with the father who comes from that past. There is also the awareness, however, that such a return is impossible.' *Father Figures: Genealogy and Narrative Structure in Rabelais* (Cornell University Press, 1991), p. 157. By analogy, we might interpret *Amadis* as a nostalgic fiction.

[16] The tactics and descriptions of the battles in Books 1 to 6 match closely with historical accounts of sixteenth-century warfare, such as that given by Bert S. Hall, *Weapons and Warfare in Renaissance Europe: Gunpowder, Technology, and Tactics* (The John Hopkins University Press, 1997).

[17] *Discours politiques et militaires*, ed. F. E. Sutcliffe (Droz, 1967), p. 175.

[18] *Le Vingt uniesme et dernier livre d'Amadis de Gaule, contenant la fin et mort d'iceluy...* There is no indication that the death of Amadis is foreseen before this point in the series. Up until this point, one supposes that Amadis will live forever.

[19] *L'Histoire Æthiopique d'Heliodorus...* (Hugues Gazeau, 1584), 'Proesme du translateur', p. 6-7.

Figure 1:
Jean Baptiste Greuze, French, 1725-1805, *Lady Reading the Letters of Heloise and Abelard*, 1758-9, oil on canvas, 81.3 x 64.8 cm © The Art Institute of Chicago, Mrs. Harold T. Martin Fund; Lacy Armour Endowment; Charles H. and Mary F.S. Worcester Collection, 1994.430.[1]

Rereading the Forbidden in *La Nouvelle Héloïse*

Ann Lewis
Queen Mary, University of London

By writing a novel, Rousseau was self-consciously (and anxiously) transgressing his own previous position regarding the value of the arts and *belles-lettres*, which he had famously condemned in the strongest possible terms. He justified himself on pragmatic grounds, notwithstanding the recognized illegitimacy of the novel form, and its dangerous effects: 'Il faut des spectacles dans les grandes villes, et des romans aux peuples corrompus. J'ai vu les mœurs de mon temps, et j'ai publié ces lettres'. To add fuel to the flames, *Julie, ou la Nouvelle Héloïse* (1761), rapidly a best-seller, is a story of forbidden love, treating the subject in unconventional ways. With its explicit reference to the letters of Heloise and Abelard which were popular and frequently re-edited in eighteenth-century France, the novel explores the (il)legitimate status of the love between Julie d'Étange and her tutor Saint-Preux - their sexual relationship forbidden by social and moral conventions, their desire to marry prohibited by Julie's father, and their love definitively outlawed when she marries the man of her father's choice. The novel captured the imagination of many eighteenth-century readers and resulted in an outpouring of emotional responses, recorded in letters to Rousseau which have themselves become famous.[2]

Instead of looking at the theme of forbidden love itself, this article will focus on the reading strategies suggested, and forbidden by the text. Rousseau's 'paratexts' draw specific attention to the problematics of reading, and his insistent attempts to direct the reader to a 'total' and linear reading paradoxically point to the interest in exploring what happens if the reader chooses not to read in this way. In particular, I will explore the effects of reading for the part rather than the whole, and of reading in reverse (changing the sequence of reading), and the functioning of 'sentimental scenes' in this context. This will serve both to re-evaluate the theme of the forbidden in the novel, and also to consider more broadly the point at which reading becomes misreading, or whether forbidden readings are necessarily 'wrong'.

*****

Paratexts

Rousseau's prefaces directly confront the issue of how *La Nouvelle Héloïse* should be read, at a number of levels.[3]   The 'first preface' concludes with two specific references to the need to read the text as a whole:

> Celle qui, malgré ce titre, en osera lire une seule page, est une fille perdue: mais qu'elle n'impute point sa perte à ce livre; le mal étoit fait d'avance. Puisqu'elle a commencé, qu'elle achève de lire: elle n'a plus rien à risquer.

> Qu'un homme austere en parcourant ce recueil se rebute aux premieres parties, jette le livre avec colere, et s'indigne contre l'Editeur; je ne me plaindrai point de son injustice; à sa place, j'en aurois pu faire autant. Que si, après l'avoir lû tout entier, quelqu'un m'osoit blamer de l'avoir publié; qu'il le dise, s'il veut, à toute la terre, mais qu'il ne vienne pas me le dire: je sens que je ne pourrois de ma vie estimer cet homme-là.[4]

This insistence can be read as an explicit instruction to the reader, even a warning, given the position of the preface just before the opening of the text. The 'Préface dialoguée' (or 'Entretien sur les romans', hereafter *Entretien*) which, unlike the first one, was originally published separately, emphasizes not only the importance of total rather than partial reading, but also the sequential aspect. To glean the 'intended' (emotional, moral) effects, the text must be read in the correct order, following the telos of the novel's plot:

> Mes jeunes gens sont aimables; mais pour les aimer à trente ans, il faut les avoir connus à vingt. Il faut avoir vécu long-temps avec eux pour s'y plaire; et ce n'est qu'après avoir déploré leurs fautes qu'on vient à goûter leurs vertus. Leurs lettres n'intéressent pas tout d'un coup; mais peu à peu elles attachent [...] C'est une longue romance dont les couplets pris à part n'ont rien qui touche, mais dont la suite produit à la fin son effet. (p. 18)

The novel's famous division into roughly two halves (before and after Julie's marriage), and the moral development this represents for the characters, underlies the repeated injunctions to read to the end, as remarked by Rousseau's interlocutor of the *Entretien*: 'Les détails de la vie domestique effacent les fautes du premier âge: la chaste épouse [...] la digne mère de famille font oublier la coupable amante' (p. 17). In fact, the *Entretien* describes the novel's moral effectiveness in terms of a 'sugared pill', by which the semi-corrupt reader, tempted by the forbidden fruit of a saucy novel will profit the most from it, undergoing (but only by reading its whole trajectory, and experiencing its full emotional charge) a conversion to virtue, a redemption, which echoes that of the heroine: 'ce même commencement doit être agéable à ceux pour qui la fin peut être utile' (p. 17).

All of which is a response to the prefatorial interlocutor's contentions that: 'la fin du recueil rend le commencement d'autant plus répréhensible; on diroit que ce sont deux livres différens que les mêmes personnes ne doivent pas lire [...] ils suceront les bords du vase, et ne boiront pas la liqueur' (p. 17). The *Entretien* therefore anticipates the heated polemics to which the novel gave rise, in which the question of unity has a central place, both in moral and aesthetic terms, and which have marked its critical history from the eighteenth century onward.

In fact, an important stage of its twentieth-century (postwar) critical history has involved the positive re-affirmation of the novel's aesthetic unity, in response to repeated moral condemnation and polemical oversimplification of its supposedly mismatched parts. In their different arguments for its unity – the integration of the 'dissertations' within its aesthetic and signifying whole, and the identification of aesthetic/thematic correspondences operating at a level other than chronology or logical argument – critics such as Coulet, Starobinski and Versini suggest the need to read for the whole on different grounds from Rousseau's moral ones.[5] Raymond's preface to the Pléiade edition makes 'lire sans sauter un seul mot' a 'condition de toute compréhension sympathique' (p. xv); for Coulet, '*La Nouvelle Héloïse* est un roman et non un recueil de textes lyriques se suffisant à eux-mêmes' (p. 379). In other words, a condition of appreciating the novel's aesthetic value – again, of reading it 'correctly' – is to read it as a whole.

*****

Part and whole

But the text lends itself to various forms of partial reading, notwithstanding Rousseau's directions, and the critical investment in 'unity'. Indeed, the ways in which fragmentary readings were used as a polemical weapon in the (often personalized) attacks on the novel, should not, by their hostility, make us overlook the ways in which the text <u>itself</u> allows us to decompose it – a forbidden reading which is not necessarily wrong.

In addition to the thematic division into halves, and the six 'parties', the novel's epistolary form lends itself to a variety of fragmentary reading strategies. Duchesne's addition of a 'table des matières' made it all the easier to select and reread particular letters, seeking effects which might be other than strict moral edification, as one disquieted male reader observed: 'Votre preface monsieur a fait L'effet que vous en attendiés, elle a piqué la Curiosité des femmes, elles ont toutes lu votre Heloyze mais elles en sont restées au Cabinet et a La 55ᵉ Lettre du premier Livre. Ainsi si votre dessein était de Les Conduire à la vertu par Le Crime, votre espérance est vaine.'[6]

The novel's self-proclaimed 'dissertations' on a range of moral and philosophical subjects were also easy to detach.[7] D'Alembert noted his preference for these parts, considered in their own right, but suggested that as such, they detracted from the 'whole': 'les details sur l'économie domestique, sur les plaisirs de la Campagne, sur l'Education &c. que L'auteur a semés dans son ouvrage, <u>me plaisent infiniment en eux-mêmes</u>, mais me paraissent réfroidir un peu l'intérêt, parce que l'unité est pour moi la première qualité des Romans' (*CC*, VIII, pp. 341-2).

The novel's 'sentimental scenes' are a privileged example of 'detachable' parts – read and reread with pleasure and *attendrissement*, and forming an affective core. While the term *tableau* referred to a range of descriptive and metaphorical as well as pictorial functions: 'Dans la multitude des tableaux de différente espece qu'il se plait à rassembler, soit qu'il peigne la simplicité respectable des mœurs Valesanes, [...] ou l'impatience effrené de l'amour qui attend le bonheur',[8] the text also includes a series of verbal *scènes* or *spectacles*, for which the painterly and theatrical models were recognized.[9] The emotional effects of internal *spectacles*, is emphatic: 'O spectacle! ô regrets! Je me sentois déchirer de douleur et transporter de joye' (p. 422); 'ô spectacle de volupté...' (p. 147); 'du plus attendrissant de tous les spectacles' (p. 322). Indeed it was the combined effect of their emotional or inflammatory charge (particularly the scenes in the first parts of the novel) and their easy detachability which had so worried the marquis de La Guerche (see above).

Frontispieces

A particularly interesting example of how scenes could be selected, detached and re-ordered (and one which has received almost no critical attention) is in their appearance in different frontispieces to the novel and Rousseau's *Oeuvres*. Marillier's four frontispieces to the 1788 *Oeuvres complètes* (Poinçot) provide a rich example of this in their complex arrangement of a selection of scenes in the form of 'medallions' (scene + *inscription*) set against a meaningful backdrop, which embody both a summary and an implicit commentary on the novel. Not only are these one of the 'non-authorized' sets of illustrations (contrasting with the 'official' Gravelot ones), but, because they generally avoid duplication with the Moreau series also included in the 1788 edition, they provide an unusual selection, suggesting forbidden readings in various ways.

The first frontispiece includes an impressively transgressive set of images – although the *baiser du bosquet* is absent (it is in the Moreau series), the selection includes most of the significant moments in the plot of Julie's 'fall' – her *aveu* ('O Dieu! suis-je assez humiliée je t'écris à genoux'), her despondency after their first sexual encounter, espied by Saint-Preux ('Que devins-je en entrouvant la porte?'); the famous *cabinet* scene while he awaits Julie ('Quel bonheur d'avoir trouvé de l'encre et du papier!'), and even a depiction of the lovers in bed representing the 'nuit inconcevable' ('Quel calme dans tous mes sens')![10] In addition, the voyeuristic aspect of the *jeu de regards* characterising many of the scenes is brought strongly into relief by Saint-Preux with his telescope on the left side of the frontispiece (see Figure 2). Two further medallions include internal voyeurs, and Saint-Preux's description of the Valaisanes ('Je recevois leur service en silence') contains an oblique voyeuristic allusion – it is the moment in the text he admits to noticing their ample breasts, and having mentally undressed Julie in the past. Finally, the representation of Julie and her father 'Je penchai mon visage sur son visage vénérable' is remarkable insofar as it depicts the moment identified by modern critics as taboo (when she is awkwardly sitting on his lap, following his attack)[11] rather than the other dramatic moments of their relationship usually depicted in eighteenth-century illustrations of the novel.

The third frontispiece (see Figure 3) includes a summary of key scenes from the fourth and fifth parts, including many of the exemplary domestic scenes (e.g. the *matinée à l'anglaise*, Saint-Preux's introduction to the children), and 'trials overcome' (the bosquet 'profané', and the crisis at Meillerie surmounted). But perhaps a key to the whole frontispiece lies in the almost hidden inscription at the bottom: 'Voici pourtant des prisonniers' – referring to the scene in the *Elysée* where Saint-Preux queries the status of the birds and fish kept captive. Although he is satisfied with the replies received in the text, the inscription of the frontispiece could suggest a wider application which insidiously undermines the exemplary status of the medallions superimposed on it. A forbidden reading?

*****

Untying the plot

Not only does the text lend itself to the forms of fragmentation outlined above, through its incorporation of easily identifiable and extractable units, but in addition, the overall structure and narrative technique of the novel serve to lessen the links holding the parts together, and to encourage readerly freedom to navigate the text in different ways. Throughout the whole novel, suspense and dramatic tension, which serve to propel the reader forward, are deliberately underplayed, together with a minimization of 'events'. The preface draws attention to this aspect of the text, while self-consciously exaggerating the point: 'Quant à l'intérêt, il est pour tout le monde, il est nul. Pas une mauvaise action; pas un méchant homme qui fasse craindre pour les bons [...] point de coup de Théatre. Tout est prévu long-temps d'avance; tout arrive comme il est prévu' (*Entretien*, p. 13).

For example, Julie's father's announcement that she must marry Wolmar (I, 28), which precipitates the consummation of her relationship with Saint-Preux, is then hardly mentioned again (and barely impinges on the lovers' consciousness) until the crisis at the very end of part one (I, 62-3) considerably reducing the dramatic conflict which would be expected to increase plot tension. The tendency for narrative self-containment of episodes rather than the development of suspense across letters, and the elimination of uncertainty before an event is even described can be illustrated by Saint-Preux's introduction of the dangerous moment on the lake: 'Je veux, Milord, vous rendre compte d'un danger que nous courumes ces jours passés, <u>et dont heureusement</u>

nous avons été quites pour la peur et un peu de fatigue.' (p. 514) Similarly, although it is true that the characters consistently try to analyse how well they are dealing with the situation of Saint-Preux's reintegration at Clarens (often formulated as the progress of Wolmar's 'cure'), it is only in Julie's posthumous letter that an element of suspense is reintroduced: 'Un jour de plus, peut-être, et j'étois coupable!' (p. 741), where her virtuous conduct (although perhaps not her feelings) was never really in doubt for the reader in the narration of events up to that point.[12]

The static 'sentimental scenes' and lengthy 'dissertations' have an important role in this tendency to narrative immobility, and in the breaking down of narrative cause and effect. Since they narrate the development of feelings and themes rather than events, they could be multiplied ad infinitum, undermining the reader's sense of a necessary movement from one to the other, or the need to read onwards in this way.[13]

Despite his partisan view, Grimm usefully draws attention to these narrative aspects, in ways which confirm the relationship between the episodic structure and the potential lack of suspense/reading momentum: 'Aucun des évenemens de ce roman n'est nécessaire [...] il est impossible qu'il y ait de l'intérêt lorsqu'il n'y a point de nécessité dans les evenemens [...] Rien ne prouve mieux la pauvreté de tête que ce renouvellement d'incidens sans aucune liaison entre eux.'[14] The present analysis is not intended as a criticism of the novel's formal structure (à la Grimm), but simply to show the ways in which the novel itself contributes to its own potential fragmentation.[15]

Changing the sequence: Rereading the forbidden

The text's capacity to splinter into autonomous fragments, and the potential unravelling of the plot movement driving the reader forward, contribute to a dynamic and unstable 'whole', allowing multiple possible trajectories, beginnings and endings. Voltaire's identification of the possibility of cutting off at different points is clearly a reductive strategy:

> Julie [...] donne à son maître un baiser très-long & très-*âcre* [...] le lendemain le maître fait un enfant à l'écolière. Les Dames pourraient croire que c'est-là la conclusion du Roman: mais [...] ce Roman Philosophique dure encor cinq Tomes entiers après la conclusion. (p. 13)

Voila encore le Roman fini, à moins que Jean-Jacques ne répare la perte du faux germe, & ne fasse un second enfant à sa Suissesse. (p. 17)[16]

But Starobinski's subtle reading of the totality: 'Le roman nous offre ainsi le spectacle d'une dialectique qui aboutit à une synthèse',[17] is also forced into the parenthetical admission that there is more than one ending, or synthesis: '(Cette synthèse est formulée dans le cinquième livre, lequel peut être considéré comme une première conclusion de La Nouvelle Héloïse, d'où rebondira l'épisode final aboutissant à la mort de Julie)' (p. 109) - 'A ce bonheur terrestre, qui aurait pu être la conclusion «raisonnable» de La Nouvelle Héloïse, Rousseau oppose une seconde conclusion, qui, elle, est d'ordre religieux' (p. 140). The text demands constant re-evaluation, as it goes beyond each possible end point. But it also suggests a more radical re-reading, a retrospective reading strategy, starting from the end and moving backwards, or, in the freedom and instability created by the text's fragmented surface, allowing a ricochet of different reading possibilities.

These possibilities are not only a phenomenological process (as described by Labrosse), a critical reflex by which themes are gathered together (Séité), or the aesthetic appreciation of a 'rêve éveillé' (Starobinski) – they also imply an interpretative value. While Rousseau's instructions insist on the need to read the whole novel, in the right order, to glean the right moral conclusion, the text suggests a range of forbidden reading strategies, which in turn suggest a rereading of the issues of legitimacy and value which underpin the novel's structure.

Symptomatic of a wider process, Julie's several letters of recapitulation – written after her marriage (III,18, 20) and just before her death (VI, 12) – provide the reader with hinges on which the reading process can be redirected, while themselves also being subject to critical re-reading. Letter III, 18 consists of a change in discourse on Julie's part by which she accommodates her change in status. While the recapitulation is presented as a revelation, filling in the gaps missing from the story so far ('pour expliquer ce que ma conduite eut toujours d'obscur à vos yeux', p. 340), her description of 'providence éternelle': 'Qui m'a mise sous la sauvegarde d'un époux vertueux, sage [...] Qui me permet, enfin, d'aspirer encore au titre d'honnête femme [...] la main secourable [...] qui leve à mes yeux le voile de l'erreur, et me rend à moi malgré moi-même' (p. 356) rewrites the story of her love affair with Saint-Preux – eliding the role of her father's prejudiced interdiction, and their hopes to legitimate their love by having a child and marrying. In addition, in her following letter, passion is re-evaluated as inherently destructive, and an unsound basis for marriage ('L'amour est accompagné d'une inquiétude continuelle [...] peu convenable au mariage, qui est un état de jouissance et de paix', p. 372), and their previous love is re-qualified as 'illusion', 'égarement' and 'commerce criminel'. However, the legitimacy and 'naturalness' of their love had precisely been an important argument of the preceding sections, legitimized by Edouard's robust support, and disqualified only by the false prejudices of the baron.

This shift in interpretation, however important to Julie's peace of mind, is not necessarily accepted by the reader. The revelation of her final letter 'Je me suis longtems fait illusion' (p. 740) together with the statement 'Après tant de sacrifices je compte pour peu celui qui me reste à faire: Ce n'est que mourir une fois de plus' (p. 741) reflects not only her recognition that she had misinterpreted the nature of her continued love for Saint-Preux, but, for the reader, also initiates a more sustained reassessment of the value of the lovers' sacrifices and the virtues of family life (especially given the choice of Saint-Preux and Claire not to marry at the end of the novel – favouring a fragmenting of the community at Clarens, rather than its 'reasonable' consolidation of the family unit). This reassessment easily takes the form of the backwards glance over the problematics of the second half, the moments which modern critics have almost invariably identified. At the level of personal fulfilment, these include Julie's revelation in her penultimate letter to Saint-Preux that she was, despite everything, not happy: 'Je ne vois par tout que sujets de contentement, et je ne suis pas contente [...] Mon ami, je suis trop heureuse; le bonheur m'ennuye' (VI, 8, p. 694); the problem of Julie's opacity to herself and others given the supposed primacy accorded to 'confiance' and 'transparence' at Clarens: 'Un voile de sagesse et d'honnêteté fait tant de replis autour de son coeur, qu'il n'est plus possible à l'oeil humain d'y pénétrer, pas même au sien propre' (p. 509); to say nothing of the whole range of problematic political and social issues associated with Clarens. A chain of problems that might lead the reader back to III, 18 whose reinterpretation, claiming to throw off the illusion of love, was itself an illusion, and whose reformulated ethical position was perhaps also as flawed as this judgement.

A backwards rereading might also extend to what is not said. For example, the text's claim that none of the characters are *méchant*, could be re-evaluated. Although Wolmar is clearly not a villain in the manner of Lovelace, his claims to have acted for the best, 'saving' Julie from a no-win situation, could be reread as pure selfishness given his pre-knowledge of her love for Saint-Preux, particularly when compared with Milord Edouard's altruism in a similar situation. The key role of sentimental scenes themselves, with their hyperbolic idealization of the family, could also be re-examined critically. Occurring at key moments, these scenes serve to confirm Julie's decision to sacrifice her love (in particular, her father's pleas on bended knee - 'la force paternelle'), as well as constituting moments of exemplary familial and social interaction in parts IV and V. But these could also be reread as the means by which the cracks in the system, its repressive aspects, are insidiously papered over – is their sentimental *élan* any more than the 'guirlandes de fleurs sur les chaînes de fer' anathemized in Rousseau's critique of the sciences and arts? Their coercive (as much as compensatory) value is clear from Wolmar's deliberate stage-management of many of the scenes of the second half to further his 'cure'.[18]

The backwards reading therefore is not only the elegiac, longing glance at the 'beau rivage' of innocence, or lost love, but also a reassessment of its value, and that of the proposed syntheses of the various *dénouements* of the novel. And if this rereading is followed through, the necessity of the passage from passionate love to dutiful sacrifice and social order (requiring the severe curtailment of all forms of desire, the sublimation of passionate love into sentimental affection for family and friends)[19] might be called into question, together with the assumption made by the characters (and author?) that this transition equates to virtue.

A re-evaluation of the forbidden through a forbidden reading then, might suggest that the novel's transgression in eighteenth-century terms lies in the arguments of the first parts that innocence and (sexual) passion can co-exist (and regardless of social class),[20] and that contrary to or despite dialectical and linear readings, the 'faute' is not 'effacée' by the 'détails domestiques' but rather the reverse. The supposedly moral sections might lead to the conclusion that forbidden love is legitimate after all.

Figure 2: The first of four Marillier frontispieces devoted to *La Nouvelle Héloïse* in the 1788 Poinçot edition of the *Oeuvres complètes de J. J. Rousseau*. Reproduced by permission of the British Library [BL: 12270.p1].

Figure 3: The third frontispiece for *La Nouvelle Héloïse* in the 1788 Poinçot edition of the *Oeuvres complètes de J.J. Rousseau*. Reproduced by permission of the British Library [BL: 12270.p1].

NOTES

[1] Although the lady is clearly reading (a version of) the medieval 'Heloise', it is possible that Greuze knew of Rousseau's novel which circulated in manuscript form for several years before its publication. (See Martha Wolff, 'An early painting by Greuze and its literary associations' *Burlington Magazine*, September 1996, 580-585). The painting clearly demonstrates the ambiguous pleasures which certain reading strategies could elicit. Of course, the dangers of reading, or the trigger to erotic desire represented by reading is an internal theme in both the original Heloise and Rousseau's text, as suggested in the relationship between tutor and pupil.

[2] On the reception of *La Nouvelle Héloïse* focusing on the correspondence, see: Anna Attridge, 'The Reception of *La Nouvelle Héloïse*' *SVEC* 120 (1974), 227-267; Robert Darnton, 'Readers Respond to Rousseau: The Fabrication of Romantic Sensitivity', in *The Great Cat Massacre and Other Episodes in French Cultural History* (Basic Books, 1984), pp. 215-256 and Claude Labrosse, *Lire au XVIIIe siècle: La Nouvelle Héloïse et ses lecteurs* (Presses Universitaires de Lyon, 1985), amongst others.

[3] Most critics have focused on the prefatorial treatment of 'authenticity', and its projection of different readers, which are not the main focus here.

[4] *Julie, ou La Nouvelle Héloïse*, in *Oeuvres complètes*, II, ed. B. Gagnebin et M. Raymond, Bibliothèque de la Pléiade (Gallimard,1964), p. 6. All further references will be to this edition. All underlining in quotations is mine.

[5] Henri Coulet, *Le Roman jusqu'à la révolution*, 9th edn (Colin, 2000), pp. 367-382; Jean Starobinski, *Jean-Jacques Rousseau. La Transparence et l'obstacle: Suivi de sept essais sur Rousseau* (Gallimard, 1971); Laurent Versini, 'Le roman épistolaire symphonique et total', in *Le Roman épistolaire* (PUF, 1979), pp. 84-99.

[6] Louis-François de Bruc de Montplaisir, marquis de La Guerche, à Rousseau, (3 mai 1761), in *Correspondance complète de Rousseau*, ed. R. A. Leigh (University of Wisconsin Press, 1969), VIII, p. 316. All further references will be to *CC*.
  For an account of the novel's libertine reception through 'lectures parcellaires', see Tanguy l'Aminot, 'Julie libertine' *Etudes Jean-Jacques Rousseau* 5 (1991), 99-126. For a detailed account of the role of the 'table des matières', together with a consideration of the specifically distancing and intellectualizing effects of partial (re)readings, see Yannick Séité, *Du livre au lire: La Nouvelle Héloïse, roman des Lumières* (Champion, 2002).

[7] Parts of the novel were literally detached and re-edited in other collections of texts e.g. *Essays on suicide, and the immortality of the soul by the late David Hume, Esq.* [...] *To which is added, Two letters on suicide, from Rosseau's* [sic] *Eloisa.* (Smith, 1783). Labrosse (1985) analyses several *ouvrages d'extraits*, including Formey's attempt to remove all scandalous parts: *L'Esprit de Julie ou extrait de la Nouvelle Héloïse, ouvrage utile à la société et particulièrement à la jeunesse* (1763).

[8] *Journal des savants, CC*, VIII, p. 351.

[9] Jean-Pierre Preudhome, Greuze's student, wrote to Rousseau: 'il [Greuze] peint comme vous Ecrivez', (12 avril 1763), *CC*, XVI, p. 58. See also Michel Lioure, 'La Nouvelle Héloïse et le théâtre' *EJJR* (1991), 45-52. The detachability and autonomous status of such scenes was reinforced by their repeated illustration by different artists throughout the

eighteenth and nineteenth centuries, following Rousseau's original commission of the Gravelot series.

[10] This is reminiscent of Crébillon fils's very selective textual compilation of letter-fragments in *Le Temple de Vénus* ([n.pub.], 1777) by which the plot is reduced to the seduction of Julie, culminating in the 'nuit inconcevable'.

[11] See Tony Tanner, *Adultery in the Novel: Contract and Transgression* (Johns Hopkins University Press, 1979), pp. 113-178, and Peggy Kamuf, *Fictions of Feminine Desire: Disclosures of Heloise* (University of Nebraska Press, 1982), pp. 97-122.

[12] There are some exceptions – Julie's 'chagrin secret' (eventually revealed as Wolmar's atheism) is mentioned and left unexplained in a way which does create suspense.

[13] Scenes such as Saint-Preux's enjoyment of the spectacle of Julie and Claire's embrace (I,38), the *matinée à l'anglaise* (V,3), or *fête des vendanges* (V,7), could be amplified and multiplied endlessly – they are not 'necessary' to plot movement.

[14] Grimm (15 janvier 1761), *CC*, VIII, pp. 344-5. His ironic critique also plays on the question of narrative causality by repeatedly implying that the cause of each narrative event is Rousseau's desire to insert a dissertation.

[15] Clearly, the novel was also read continuously - many contemporary accounts describe its consumption at speed, implying a degree of suspense. Nonetheless, the examples outlined above demonstrate a perceived relationship between certain kinds of fragment, the lack of 'necessity', and a slowing of *intérêt*.

[16] *Lettres sur La Nouvelle Héloïse ou Aloisa de Jean Jacques Rousseau, Citoyen de Genève* ([n.pub.], 1761); [BL: 11805.cc.34 (2)].

[17] 'Un double *non* a été prononcé, mais qui a permis de dire tour à tour *oui* au désir et *oui* à la vertu./ Ce que l'on retrouve sur un plan supérieur, c'est une nouvelle société et un nouvel amour [...]. L'exigence érotique et l'exigence d'ordre sont finalement reconciliées', *Transparence*, p. 109.

[18] It should be noted that my forbidden reading in this paragraph reflects a modern perspective. However widely the novel's *vertu* was interpreted in the eighteenth century, the sentimental myth of family values was certainly not deconstructed in this way. Interestingly, several recent readings of the family in *La Nouvelle Héloïse* have focused on the incest taboo (Tanner (1979) and Kamuf (1982) in terms of the 'father's desire', and Anne Deneys-Tunney, in an examination Saint-Preux's desire for 'the mother', *Ecritures du corps: De Descartes à Laclos*, PUF, 1992, pp. 193-265), again showing how far readings of, and definitions of what is 'forbidden' are historically changeable.

[19] A developmental necessity replicated in many of Rousseau's other texts, and confirmed most violently in *Le Lévite d'Ephraïm*, where the possibility of achieving social harmony is predicated on the necessity of women's (virtuous) sacrifice of passion for family and community. (See also Judith Still, 'Rousseau's *Lévite d'Ephraïm*: The imposition of meaning (on women)', *French Studies* XLIII (1989), 12-30.)

[20] 'Mes tableaux voluptueux auroient perdu toutes leurs graces si le doux coloris de l'innocence y eut manqué', *Confessions*, *OC*, I, p. 435.

'Leur bouche est en paroles aussi honnêtes que le trou de mon cul': Cynic Freedom of Speech in French Texts, 1581-1615

Hugh Roberts
Oxford Brookes University

When asked what was the most beautiful thing in the world, Diogenes the Cynic replied, 'freedom of speech' (*parrhesia*).[1] Diogenes, of the fourth century BC, was the archetypal Cynic of antiquity. He gained notoriety for his odd mixture of asceticism, shamelessness, and ready wit. According to Diogenes Laertius, whose *Lives of Eminent Philosophers* (third century AD) is the most important source for early modern and modern knowledge of the Cynics, Diogenes lived in a large wine-jar, openly masturbated in the market place and told the most powerful man in the world, Alexander the Great, to get out of the way of his sun.[2] Diogenes' encounters with the powerful are paradigmatic instances of *parrhesia*, since they involve telling the truth when this entails putting oneself in great danger.[3] Diogenes has licence to say what is normally forbidden because he demonstrates his freedom from social constraints, and commitment to nature, through performative use of his body.[4] Freedom of speech is always linked to the body, including its most basic functions, both because freedom of speech follows from shamelessness and because the *parrhesiast* is risking life and limb. The Cynics also use *parrhesia* as a heuristic device to persuade others to return to a natural kind of living.[5] Freedom of speech is a vital part of the Cynics' frequently humorous philosophical performance. Humour is not incidental to Cynicism, but rather Diogenes' jokes, such as telling a king to get out of the way so as he might continue sunbathing, invariably involve subverting unarticulated conventions.[6]

My subject is not, however, Cynic freedom of speech *per se*, but the responses to, and uses of, *parrhesia* in French texts of the late-sixteenth and early-seventeenth-century. It is no surprise to discover that Cynic freedom of speech resonated at this time of religious conflict and persecution in western Europe. Precisely because freedom of speech could be thought of as a broad phenomenon, I shall restrict my discussion to *prima facie* references to the Cynics which employ *parrhesia* in some way. This is not however the same thing as saying that sixteenth-century French texts are Cynical themselves. Rather, if they are of any autonomous interest at all, it is because they adapt, and improvise upon, the Cynic performance of *parrhesia*. I shall examine a range of these adaptations in a varitey of texts, including, most importantly, a political poem from the Spanish Netherlands, Montaigne's *Essais*, and Béroalde de Verville's *Le Moyen de parvenir*. Echoes of Cynic freedom of speech serve as a guide to a few of the ways in which this period imagined radical opposition to the political and social status quo.

The most spectacular use of the figure of Diogenes for political ends in this period was made by an anonymous Flemish author writing in French. His *Diogènes, ou du moïen d'establir, après tant de misères et de calamitez, une bonne et asseurée paix en France, et la rendre plus florissante qu'elle ne fust jamais* (Liège: 1581) is an appeal to the French to intervene in the Netherlands against the repressive policies of Philip II.[7] The lengthy poem is written in the voice of Diogenes, who famously sought, with a lighted lantern in the midday sun, for a man in a crowd.[8] It begins thus:

> Scauriez vous poinct Messieurs (mais quil ne vous desplaise)
> Ou je pourroy trouver, dont je suis à malaise
> Ung homme de vertu, de bons sens, & de cœur,
> Qui voulust s'opposer à ce tyran vainqueur (p. 2)

Diogenes' paradoxical quest is refashioned as a search for true Frenchmen who would stand up to the Spanish monarch ('ce tyran vainqueur'). Unsurprisingly, the audience laughs at Diogenes' antics with the lantern, but the poet points out that they require this bizarre visual aid, because they are blind to the dangers they face: 'Et certes, puisque goute/Ne voïez à midy, c'est raison que j'adjouste/Ce secours à voz yeulx' (p. 3). Diogenes' lantern here shines with the light of unpalatable truth. It is plain that the author of this remarkable piece chose Diogenes neither for his shamelessness nor his wit, but because he stands for truth and freedom in opposition to political oppression. This leads to an idealization of the Cynic. In the final lines of the poem, following Diogenes' speech and his disappearance, the poet wonders whether it was a 'homme mortel ou quelque ange céleste?' but in any case concludes that 'François, c'est Dieu, par luy, qui vous parle et proteste' (p. 58). Such a rose-tinted presentation of the Cynic is in part a predictable result of turning him into a political mouthpiece. Nonetheless, it also fits into a tradition dating back to antiquity, in which the Cynics are idealized in order to be appropriated to non-Cynic ideological ends.[9] In this instance, it is plain that the political points the poem makes have little, if anything, to do with Cynicism. This does not, however, obscure the vital fact that a version of Diogenes was chosen to make them, showing that Cynic freedom of speech could be turned into a powerful rhetorical tool at this time. That the views expressed in the poem were dangerous means that the poem as a whole can be seen as an example of *parrhesia*, making Diogenes an appropriate choice to be its spokesman.

While *Diogènes, ou du moïen d'establir* shows that Cynic anecdote could be used for subversive purposes, most representations of Cynic *parrhesia* are far less radical. The encounter between Diogenes and Alexander was so easily presented in an unthreatening way that it became a commonplace. This is seen, for example, in the second book of Guillaume Bouchet's dialogue *Les Sérées* (1597) in which one of the speakers remarks 'Je ne diray point [...] pour estre trop commun, la liberté de parler de Diogenes à Alexandre', although, despite saying this, he proceeds to relate the various relevant anecdotes at length.[10] Similarly, in Jean-Pierre Camus's mammoth miscellany, *Les Diversitez* (1609-18), the reader is informed, in a chapter entitled 'Du parler libre', that 'Ceste franchise de parler du Philosophe Diogenes à Alexandre est cognuë aux enfans'.[11] Camus gives a rare definition of *parrhesia*: 'une façon de parler brusque, naïsve, prompte, qui a bien de verité quelque air d'inconsideration & legereté, mais qui part d'un courage boussy, de je ne sçay quelle fierté genereuse, dédaignant toute adstriction & circonspection' (fol. 117ᵛ). Despite acknowledging the courage and naturalness of freedom of speech, Bishop Camus finds it hard to take Diogenes seriously: 'il y a en toutes ses actions, tant de vanité & de sottise qu'à peine me semble-il meriter le nom de Philosophe, si ce n'est pour quelques reparties visves & promptes, & autres apophtegmes qu'on luy attribue, qui encores considerez attentivement, ont plus du basteleresque que du serieux'.[12] Camus does not get the Cynic's jokes, thereby missing the point of his seriocomic philosophical performance.

Despite its commonplace status, the anecdote about Diogenes and Alexander could still be adapted in interesting ways by skilled writers. This is true of Montaigne's short essay, 'De Democritus et Heraclitus' (I, 50).[13] The pairing of Democritus, who laughed at the nature of mankind, and Heraclitus, who wept at the same thing, is one of the most widespread *topoi* of the sixteenth century. Montaigne maintains that laughter is preferable to tears, since the former is more scathing than the latter. Diogenes is cited on the side of Democritus as an example of someone who scorned the vanity of human existence:

> [A] Ainsi Diogenes, qui baguenaudoit apart soy, roulant son tonneau et hochant du nez le grand Alexandre, nous estimant des mouches ou des vessies pleines de vent, estoit bien juge plus aigre et plus poingnant, et par consequent plus juste, à mon humeur, que Timon, celuy qui fut surnommé le haisseur des hommes. (I, 50, 303-04)

Montaigne chooses his words with care: the verb 'baguenauder', which means to fool around, like children who burst the pods of the bladder senna (*le baguenaudier*), is closely echoed by the 'vessies pleines de vent'. Diogenes takes a pin to human vanity, cocking a snook ('hochant du nez') at the world's most powerful man. Montaigne thereby characterizes Diogenes as a kind of wise fool, who demonstrates his contempt for the normal run of men through bizarre, childlike performance, which involves his body, props (his barrel-rolling, which is a reference to Rabelais's portrayal of Diogenes in the prologue of the *Tiers Livre*) and *parrhesia*. The representation of Diogenes here is inevitably unlike that demanded by the political nature of *Diogènes, ou du moïen d'establir*, showing that many different Cynics can be fashioned out of the ancient and early-modern sources. Far from expressing divine truth, Diogenes' freedom of speech in this passage is one strand of his seriocomic performance as a philosophical jester.

Cynic freedom of speech is treated in yet further ways in 'L'Apologie de Raimond Sebond', Montaigne's longest and most complex essay. The first example is found in the context of a discussion

of religion from its opening pages. Montaigne's argument is already outspoken: observing that people twist Scripture to their own ends, he goes
on to suggest that '[C] Il n'est point d'hostilité excellente comme la
chrestienne' and that 'Nostre religion est faicte pour extirper les vices,
elle les couvre, les nourrit, les incite' (II, 12, 444). This in turn leads to a
discussion of blasphemy which, Montaigne observes, is attractive
because the forbidden is accompanied by a frisson of pleasure.
Montaigne's thesis is forthright, powerful, and consistent. However, the
reference to two Cynics that immediately follows it troubles any
straightforward reading:

> [C] Le philosophe Antisthenes, comme on l'initioit aux mysteres
> d'Orpheus, le prestre luy disant que ceux qui se voüoyent à cette
> religion avoyent à recevoir apres leur mort des biens eternels et
> parfaicts: Pourquoy ne meurs tu donc toi mesmes? luy fit-il.
> Diogenes, plus brusquement selon sa mode, et hors de nostre
> propos, au prestre qui le preschoit de mesme de se faire de son
> ordre pour parvenir aux biens de l'autre monde: Veux tu pas que
> je croye qu'Agesilaüs et Epaminondas, si grands hommes, seront
> miserables, et que toy, qui n'es qu'un veau, seras bien heureux
> par ce que tu es prestre? (II, 12, 444)[14]

These anecdotes could be seen as an illustration of the pleasure of
blasphemy, or of challenging authority. However, the witty *parrhesia* of
the Cynics here is positive, whereas blasphemy is obviously negative.
Montaigne remarks that Diogenes' put-down is 'hors de nostre propos',
thus signaling a digression. Yet this digression still implies the reverse of
what was being argued previously. Moreover, in Diogenes Laertius, there
is no mention of a priest in the second anecdote. Rather, it is the people
of Athens who want Diogenes to be initiated. Montaigne, in inventing the
priest, specifically characterizes Diogenes' repartee as being disregard
for religion, rather than civil disobedience. The Cynics' outspoken
disrespect for the promises of religion could be seen as hinting at an
atheistic subtext to what Montaigne is saying here. However, it is more
likely that the priests in the two anecdotes represent the mass of
supposed believers whose actions fail to match their beliefs. The Cynic
anecdotes are nonetheless unsettling. Like much of the *Apologie*, and the

Essais more generally, they imply an outspoken disrespect for religion and spiritual mystery. However, this disrespect never falls into outright atheism. Montaigne thereby uses the Cynics to explore a taboo area whilst he simultaneously remains within the boundaries of those same taboos.

A different kind of freedom of speech is seen in an encounter between Diogenes' best-known disciple, Crates, and the latter's brother-in-law, Metrocles. It forms part of Montaigne's brief discussion of Cynic shamelessness toward the end of the *Apologie*, and shows how basic bodily functions can be used to make a philosophical point:

> [C] Metroclez lascha un peu indiscretement un pet en disputant, en presence de son eschole, et se tenoit en sa maison, caché de honte, jusques à ce que Crates le fut visiter; et, adjoutant à ses consolations et raisons l'exemple de sa liberté, se mettant à peter à l'envi avec luy, il luy osta ce scrupule [...] (II, 12, 583)[15]

Crates' farting demonstrates the folly of Metrocles' shame through comic use of the body, and in particular what Bakhtin calls the 'lower-body stratum'.[16] It is far more persuasive than any theoretical argument, and much of the comedy of the passage comes from the contrast between the act of breaking wind and serious 'consolations et raisons'. Crates' farts work as shockingly outspoken arguments. In much the same way as Diogenes' freedom of speech towards Alexander can be converted into an insulting gesture ('hochant du nez'), so Crates' flatulence becomes a powerful kind of rhetoric. Unlike Camus, Montaigne has recognized that the Cynics combine shameless bodily display and freedom of speech in lives devoted to heuristic performance.

The link between the body and *parrhesia* is also explored in Béroalde de Verville's enigmatic *Le Moyen de parvenir* (c.1615).[17] This work's heady combination of a great number of dirty stories with an almost postmodern distrust of the power of texts coherently to convey knowledge has given rise to a good deal of critical attention in recent years.[18] Critics are agreed that *Le Moyen* constitutes an attack on the authority of written texts. They observe that the chapter-titles bear no relation to their content, that, although supposedly a banquet, there is an implausibly large number of speakers (over four hundred), that the conversations are transcribed by an author-figure who not only mixes eveything up, but eventually joins in the dialogue himself as just another character, that readers can insert themselves or their relatives into the text. Through strategies such as these, *Le Moyen* undermines its readers' confidence in books that tell them how to think and live. This attack on the authority of the written word spreads itself to the speakers' names. These generally fail to reflect their historical characters and some speakers even bear mysterious sobriquets like 'Quelqu'un' and 'L'Autre'. The names of the interlocutors are to all intents interchangeable, their identities are therefore unstable.[19] Consequently, any authority that might have come from a given name is undermined. Yet Diogenes is something of an exception to this rule. He makes three major interventions in the dialogue, and a couple of less significant ones. More importantly, one of his interventions contains a clear allusion to the Diogenes of the tradition, and the others are Diogenic in tone and content. Diogenes' expositions on freedom of speech in *Le Moyen de parvenir* form part of its undermining of written texts, and preference for the spoken word.[20] I do not want to suggest that Diogenes is a key to this notoriously complex work, but Béroalde's rare reference to the historical character singles him out, and turns him into the obvious spokesman for freedom of speech. Kenny has shown that Béroalde, in his late works, was peculiarly interested in the topic of freedom of thought and speech, although he neglects the role of Diogenic *parrhesia* in *Le Moyen*.[21] Cynic freedom of speech is more radical than the types of 'liberté' of expression identified by Kenny (intellectual, sceptical, satirical), for it implies that telling the truth, even from the most vulnerable socio-economic position, is an ethical imperative. Since the most innocuous forms of philosophical 'liberté' give rise to anxiety, it is no surprise to discover that Béroalde does not present Cynic freedom of speech as a panacea. The ancient anecdotes relate that Alexander reacted to Diogenes' insolence by remarking that were he not Alexander, he would be Diogenes, thereby suggesting that the Cynic's self-sufficiency amounted to a kind of power comparable to his power over the world.[22] In *Le Moyen*, however, Alexander the Great would rather have given Diogenes the Cynic a beating for his lack of respect. Alexander's threat follows Diogenes' response to another speaker's complaint about the coarseness of the conversation during the banquet:

> DIOGENE - Tout est permis ici. Nous sommes pair à
> compagnon. On doit faire et dire ici tout ce qu'on peut et
> pense.
> ALEXANDRE - Vous y perdriez, pauvre homme, pource que
> si tout était permis, je vous battrais bien à ceste [gauntlet]
> pour me venger de l'affront que l'année qui vient, vous me
> fîtes en Grèce. (p. 146)

André Tournon is the only critic to have recognized that Diogenes' name
was not chosen by accident here: 'Philosophe scandaleux, exhibiant sans
vergogne sa parole et son corps affranchis de toute contrainte [...]
[Diogène] incarne la folle sagesee - ni murmure mystérieux, ni masque
de la raison critique, mais franc illogisme du plaisir' (p. viii). Although it
is true to say that Diogenes rejects both mysteries and abstract theory, I
would argue that he does not do this to embrace '[l']illogisme du plaisir',
but rather his rejection of the abstract is the other side of his commitment
to practice. Tournon rightly observes, however, that Cynic practice links
shameless bodily performance and truth-telling, as was also seen in
Montaigne's version of the encounter between Diogenes and Alexander.
Béroalde nonetheless goes beyond Montaigne and the other texts
considered above in emphasizing that the *parrhesiast* runs the risk of
violent reprimand, thereby also connecting the body with freedom of
speech. *Parrhesia* is defined in opposition to violence.[23] Alexander
stands for political and military power of the kind that can easily
endanger all kinds of freedom. In the bizarre context of *Le Moyen*,
however, the balance of power has shifted from emperor to Cynic: if
everything were indeed permitted, Alexander would have given Diogenes
a beating. This carnivalesque inversion of power is already suggested by
the ancient anecdotes, and is seen in Rabelais's Lucianic vision of Hades
in *Pantagruel*, 30, in which Diogenes is a king, giving an impoverished
Alexander a beating. In *Le Moyen*, Diogenes' plea for freedom need not
be universal, since he refers to the 'ici' of the banquet. Moreover, it is
not the noble and practical kind of freedom of *Diogènes, ou du moïen
d'establir*, but one that enables the speakers of the symposium to relate
ribald anecdotes. It may be that freedom of speech is an ideal,
particularly in the context of philosophical dialogue, but Béroalde's

adaptation of the Diogenes-Alexander anecdotes suggests that this ideal is dangerous and often impractical. Nonetheless, in a more obviously philosophical context, free-speaking is presented in an unusual but positive light. Following a spurious exposition on some 'points secrets de la profonde sagesse', Diogenes intervenes to rail against such esoteric pseudo-philosophy:

> Diogène - Que males mules aient ces philosophers foireux qui ne font qu'ânonner! Je les enverrai à mon métayer et à ses gens. Il y a plus de mille ans que le conte en est fait, mais on l'a mal retenu. La fille de ce métayer apporta des prunes à notre femme, qui lui dit: "il n'en fallait point m'amie. - C'est votre gresse, Mademeselle, prenez-les s'il vous plaît: aussi bien nos pourceaux n'en veulent point". L'après-dînée, celle de chez nous rencontra la mère de cette fille, à laquelle elle dit ce que sa fille lui avait dit. "Ardé, lui répondit-elle, Mademeselle, elle dit vrai: ces méchants pourceaux aiment mieux manger la merde". Sur le soir, je rencontrai le bonhomme, auquel je contai le tout. "Pardé! Monsieur, dit-il, ce sont bêtes: leur bouche est en paroles aussi honnêtes que le trou de mon cul". (p. 238)

Although this tale could have been told by anyone, Diogenes, whose philosophy involved mocking obscure theory through the practice of freedom of speech, is a good choice to tell it. As in Montaigne, freedom of speech is characterized as a lower bodily function, comically contrasted with supposedly high forms of discourse. *Le Moyen* in many ways exemplifies Bakhtin's notion of the carnivalesque corpus which re-asserts the body as a universal factor linking people of all backgrounds. Supposedly higher bodily functions, such as language, are inextricably tied to the body in all its earthiness. The placing of the 'lower-body stratum' over language and thought is a theme of *Le Moyen*. As one speaker puts it elsewhere, 'ce seroit belle chose de parler du cul, ce seroit un langage excellent'.[24] This lends the spoken word an unexpected kind of physicality:

Antiphon - Appelez-vous cela des paroles couvertes? Je crois qu'il les faut servir à couvert, de peur qu'elles ne s'éventent! Diogène - Si vous avez peur qu'elles s'éventent, avalez-les vitement (p. 238)

The brutally honest words of the farmer's family have become like things. They are a bodily by-product to be consumed, like the shit the pigs eat. The idea that words should be eaten to stop them from disappearing recalls the commonplace digestion metaphor for reading and writing, and in particular for the Renaissance practice of imitation.[25] The alimentary metaphor is a leitmotif of *Le Moyen*. In fact, it is taken to extremes: as one speaker puts it, the banquet becomes a banquet of words 'Je fais bonne chere de cecy, puis l'ayant digeré, je le baille à remâcher ainsi que quand j'ay bien dîné je vais fienter, et un pourceau vient qui en fait son profit' (p. 167). The *topos* of reading as digestion has been displaced onto the spoken word. Words are both excrement and foodstuff. The readers of *Le Moyen* are the pigs who eat the excrement. As the author-figure puts it, 'ceux qui ont imprimé ceci sont commissaires d'excréments: ceci est la fiente de mon esprit' (p. 295).[26] The obvious paradox in all this is that the spoken word is ephemeral, and that *Le Moyen* it is praised through writing. Nonetheless, a book that seeks to make fun of all its bookish characteristics is clearly the most appropriate place for a written exploration of the spoken word. Diogenes' anecdote implies that the freely spoken word, being the closest to thought and body, is the least ephemeral of all. Free speech is preferable to books that seek to establish some kind of authority over the world, or over other books. It is no coincidence that Diogenes, the archetypal anti-authoritan figure of antiquity, is chosen to express this view.

It is striking that there is no single way of understanding or using Cynic freedom of speech in the various texts analysed here. Such divergent perspectives show that far from being some kind of eternal idea, *parrhesia* is best thought of as a potent and provocative set of practices with great potential for adaptation. Cynic freedom of speech can be presented in such a way as to steer clear of forbidden territory, as both Bouchet and Camus demonstrate. *Diogènes, ou du moïen d'establir* is an unusual example of a Cynic performance being put to political ends, the danger of which comes close to the ancient notion of *parrhesia*. The seriousness of the poem necessitates an idealization of Diogenes, which is conspicuously absent from Montaigne's playful presentation of the Cynic, which emphasizes his witty, foolish-wise performance. Such humour, which is a vital element of the majority of the sayings and anecdotes recorded in Diogenes Laertius, is ideally suited to questioning conventions and dominant world-views, and illustrates how the forbidden can be fun. Montaigne links freedom of speech to performative use of basic bodily functions, a connection which is exploited too, but in unexpected ways, in *Le Moyen de parvenir*. While *Diogènes, ou du moïen d'establir* uses Cynic freedom of speech in response to violence and as a call to arms, Béroalde's rare reference to an historical figure, namely Diogenes, betrays his anxieties about the risk of violence run by the *parrhesiast*. Despite these concerns, *Le Moyen* presents free-speaking not as an abstract ideal but as a healthy alternative to more oppressive forms of discourse, which seek to order and control the world. Since *parrhesia* is tied to the 'lower-body stratum', it is potentially common to all people, and could by extension be used to formulate a language in which nothing was forbidden; this presumably was one of the aims of Diogenes' bizarre performance from the beginning.

NOTES

[1] Diogenes Laertius, *Lives of Eminent Philosophers*, ed. and trans. R. D. Hicks, Loeb Classical Library, 185 (Harvard University Press, 1925), VI, 69.
[2] Diogenes Laertius, VI, 23, 38 and 69.
[3] R. Bracht Branham, 'Defacing the Currency: Diogenes' Rhetoric and the *Invention* of Cynicism' in *The Cynics: The Cynic Movement in Antiquity and its Legacy*, ed. R. Bracht Branham and Marie-Odile Goulet-Cazé, Hellenistic Culture and Society, 23 (University of California Press, 1996), pp. 81-104 (pp. 96-98, and especially n.54). Foucault was working on the notion of *parrhesia* at his death, but the text of his lectures, *L'Herméneutique du sujet: cours au Collège de France, 1981-1982*, ed. François Ewald, Alessandro Fontana and Frédéric Gros (Hautes Etudes, 2001), ignores this vital aspect of *parrhesia*, recognized only in the 1983-1984 lectures (see n.28), which have yet to be published. There is however an account of these final lectures, in Thomas Flynn, 'Foucault as Parrhesiast: his Last Course at the Collège de France (1984)' in *The Final Foucault*, ed. James Bernausser and David Rasmusser (MIT Press, 1988), pp. 102-18.
[4] Branham, 'Diogenes' Rhetoric', p. 100.
[5] Flynn, 'Foucault as Parrhesiast', pp. 109-11.

[6] Branham, 'Diogenes' Rhetoric', pp. 94-99.

[7] *Recueil de poésies françoises des XVe et XVIe siècles: morales, faétieuses, historiques*, ed. M. Anatole de Montaiglon, 13 vols (A. Franck, 1855-78; repr. Kraus Reprint, 1977), IX (1865), pp. 1-58.

[8] Diogenes Laertius, VI, 41.

[9] Margarethe Billerbeck, 'The Ideal Cynic from Epictetus to Julian', *The Cynics*, pp. 205-21.

[10] *Les Sérées*, ed. C.-E. Roybet (Alphonse Lemerre, 1873; repr. Slatkine Reprints, 1969), p. 154.

[11] *Les Diversitez*, 11 vols, III (Paris: Claude Chapelet, 1610), fol. 117ᵛ. For Camus's fairly outspoken commentaries to his *histoires tragiques*, see the contribution of Marilyn Cox to this volume.

[12] *Les Diversitez*, IX (Paris: Claude Chapelet, 1616), p. 57.

[13] *Les Essais*, ed. Pierre Villey and V.-L. Saulnier, 2nd edn (Presses Universitaires de France, 1992).

[14] Diogenes Laertius, VI, 4 and 39.

[15] Diogenes Laertius, VI, 94.

[16] Mikhail Bakhtin, *Rabelais and his World*, trans. Hélène Iswolsky (Indiana University Press, 1984), *passim*.

[17] *Le Moyen de parvenir*, ed. Hélène Moreau and André Tournon (Université de Provence, Service des Publications, 1984).

[18] Michel Renaud, *Pour une lecture du Moyen de parvenir de Béroalde de Verville*, 2nd edn, (Honoré Champion, 1997); Michel Jeanneret, 'Le centre de tous les livres', *Des mets et des mots: banquets et propos de table à la Renaissance* (José Corti, 1987), pp. 221-44; Neil Kenny, *The Palace of Secrets: Béroalde de Verville and Renaissance Conceptions of Knowledge* (Oxford University Press, 1991), pp. 8, 82-85, 118-25, 142-55, 206-07, 238; Barbara Bowen, '*Le Moyen de parvenir*: the Name of the Game', *Words and the Man in French Renaissance Literature* (French Forum, 1983), pp. 111-28.

[19] Kenny, *Palace of Secrets*, p. 145.

[20] Bowen, *Words and the Man*, pp. 125-28.

[21] Neil Kenny, '"Car le nom mesme de liberalité sonne liberté": les contextes sociaux et économiques du savoir chez Béroalde de Verville', *Béroalde de Verville 1556-1626*, Cahiers V.-L. Saulnier, 13 (Presses de l'École Normale Superieure, 1996), pp. 7-24.

[22] Diogenes Laertius, VI, 32.

[23] Kenny, '"Car le nom mesme de liberalité sonne liberté"', p. 18.

[24] Chap. 41, Jeanneret, 'Le centre de tous les livres', p. 238.

[25] Jeanneret, 'Le centre de tous les livres', pp. 234-38

[26] See *Essais*, III, 9, 946.

PART II:
IMAGES OF THE FORBIDDEN AND FORBIDDEN IMAGES

Portraits photographiques de femmes voilées et dévoilées : pratiques, expériences et lectures transgressives à partir des trois points de vue proposés par Roland Barthes, dans *La Chambre claire*

Catherine Guy-Murrell
University of Reading

Aujourd'hui, la photographie ne peut plus entretenir l'illusion d'un regard objectif de l'objectif. On sait depuis la publication de *On Photography* de Susan Sontag que les photographies sont plus précisément des 'artifacts', qui mêlent 'the real', informations et réalités, et 'fantasy', fantaisies et fantasmes.[1] On sait aussi empiriquement qu'au XXIè siècle, la photographie est devenue à la fois, un art et un médium privilégié, dans nos sociétés grandes consommatrices d'images. Là, la puissance du symbole, si elle n'est que peu souvent analysée, reste fortement codifiée. Dans la période de l'après 11 septembre 2001 et particulièrement à travers les images de femmes afghanes abondamment diffusées, le voile est devenu, en occident, un symbole-écran mythifié par deux siècles d'orientalisme et mystificateur d'une double réalité féminine et musulmane que l'on croit connaître.[2]

J'ai appris en visitant l'exposition *Veil*[3], un projet conçu et developpé par Zineb Sedira et Jananne Al-Ani, deux artistes d'origine arabe qui vivent et travaillent à Londres, qu'il n'y a pas de mot arabe pour le voile. Il y a cependant des voiles : tchador, burkha, haïk, hidjab, qui correspondent à des pratiques, des formes et des couleurs variant constamment selon les traditions géographiques, religieuses et politiques, à des moments précis de l'histoire. Au Maghreb, dont il sera plus particulièrement question ici, les voiles traditionnels sont : le haïk et le hidjab (connu en France sous l'étiquette de foulard islamique).[4]

Aujourd'hui, dans une perspective postcoloniale toujours binaire et déterminée à percer le mystère de l'orient musulman, si le voile est assimilé globalement à l'institution islamique et à son fanatisme, il s'inscrit aussi dans une symbolique de la résistance traversant plusieurs générations de Maghrébines et s'assimilant souvent à une lutte politique identitaire à travers la colonisation, la décolonisation, la nationalisation, la révolution, l'occidentalisation et l'anti-occidentalisation. De façon sommaire, le mythe et la résistance semblent s'organiser autour d'un mélange de fétichisme et de subordination, entre la 'local patriarchy' et l' 'international politics'.

La multitude d'analyses existantes reflètant la complexité grandissante du voile-sujet[5], j'ai préféré ne pas me confiner au rêve européen *fin de siècle* qui dévoile mais plutôt adopter, à sa place, trois expériences photographiques proposées par Roland Barthes : ' [...] une photo peut être l'objet de trois pratiques (ou de trois émotions, ou de trois intentions) : faire, subir, regarder. L'*Operator*, c'est le Photographe. Le *Spectator*, c'est nous tous qui compulsons, dans les journaux, les livres, les albums, les archives, des collections de photos. Et celui ou cela qui est photographié, c'est la cible [...]'.[6] Ce que m'a révélé cette étude, ce sont une pratique, une expérience et un discours, qui, aux trois époques étudiées : les années 1920, 1960 et 2000, transforment l'image, encouragent des alternatives, banissent la polarisation binaire est/ouest et facilitent le dialogue pluridisciplinaire et multiculturel, par la transgression des conventions établies.

Le point de vue de l'*Operator*[7] qui regarde la femme voilée

Dans *La Chambre claire*, Roland Barthes écarte rapidement le point de vue du photographe sous prétexte qu'il n'est pas lui-même adepte de la pratique photographique : '[...] la Photographie de l'*Operator* était liée au contraire à la vision découpée par le trou de la serrure de la *camera obscura*. Mais de cette émotion-là (ou cette essence) je ne pouvais parler, ne l'ayant jamais connue; je ne pouvais rejoindre la cohorte de ceux (les plus nombreux) qui traitent de la Photo-selon-le Photographe.' (p.24).[8]

Lorsqu'il s'agit de la représentation visuelle de la femme musulmane, il m'a semblé au contraire intéressant d'étudier brièvement deux démarches de photographes qui défient, à presque un siècle d'intervalle, à la fois la forme, les normes esthétiques de la photographie, et le fond, les tabous culturels et idéologiques, en vigueur. La première est celle de Gatian de Clérambault, au début du XXè siècle, la seconde celle de Majida Khattari, en 2001.

Gaëtan Gatian de Clérambault était photographe et psychiatre.[9] Blessé au front en 1917, il fut nommé médecin-major, en poste à Fez. Entre 1918 et 1934, il y photographia des centaines de sujets voilés d'un haïk recouvrant entièrement le corps et le visage.[10] On sait peu de choses sur les circonstances dans lesquelles ces photographies furent prises; on connaît, cependant, leurs petites tailles (16 x 23 cm ou 28 x 39 cm) et le fait qu'elles furent souvent constituées en séries.

Ces clichés se distinguent clairement des images stéréotypées orientalistes qui dominaient la photographie, au début du XXè siècle. Clérambault ne choisit pas la photo-tableau commerciale en studio, mais, au contraire, soit des intérieurs authentiques [Pl. I], soit des extérieurs naturels. Il représente donc des femmes actives, dans leurs environnements, ce qui contraste nettement avec l'imagerie dominante de la représentation féminine, qui préfèrait la femme orientale voilée, en situation de pose figée, passive et prête à être dévoilée par le spectateur européen voyeur et fétichisant, en position de supériorité.

En l'absence de visage ou de regard, toute l'intentionnalité étant dirigée sur le vêtement, la démarche de Clérambault correspond à 'the act of veiling itself' et montre un certain respect du voile, qui cache et protège l'intimité du sujet.[11] Je note, dans le même sens, le titre qui accompagne les photos : 'Etudes sur l'étoffe' et en déduit que le sujet est bien le drappé ou voile-enveloppe que Clérambault voulait cachant mais aussi mouvant et changeant, plein de vie comme les Marocaines photographiées.

Si cette focalisation sur le voile n'est pas disputée par le psychiatre Serge Tisseron, ce dernier voit aussi, sous l'étoffe, la menace de certains gestes ou mouvements du corps [Pl. II] et, dans la fente noire à la hauteur des yeux tournée vers l'objectif, l'énigme inquiétante d'un regard justement sans yeux [Pl. III]. En ce qui concerne les mouvements du drappé, souvent discrets au point d'être presque imaginés, Tisseron les assimile dans leur dynamique, à un langage de la peau dans lequel les plis du tissu correspondraient, par exemple, aux rides, sur la peau d'une femme supposée agée.[12] Quant au regard absent, Tisseron analyse ici l'acte photographique comme la manifestation d'une fascination énigmatique et obsessionnelle de l'*Operator* pour un sujet 'image inquiétante d'un autre' transmise au *Spectator*, par la photo.[13] L'aspect de 'présence quasiment hallucinatoire' d'une telle image se manifeste plus particulièrement et paradoxalement quand et parce que le regard n'est pas renvoyé. Le voile devient, dans cette analyse, un 'prétexte à un questionnement autour du miroir' qui réactive 'l'ambiguïté dont est porteuse la première image de soi' dans le miroir.[14]

Revenons-en aux séries de photos et à un autre type d'angoisse. Les modifications de positions du modèle restent très légères d'une photo à l'autre et le sujet tourne souvent le dos à l'objectif. Les attributs féminins (cheveux et poitrine) ayant souvent été dissimulés sous le voile, la question de savoir s'il s'agit du même sujet et d'un sujet féminin reste, pour moi, doublement équivoque. Une observation prolongée m'encourage à passer du mystère à l'angoisse et à faire le lien entre ce que Laura Mulvey appelle la 'sexuality of surface' du visuel et la 'topography of the phantasmatic space' de l'imaginaire, pour lire, sous couvert chez Clérambault, 'a deep-seated anxiety about the female body'.[15]

En matière de représentation visuelle du voile islamique, la seconde artiste, qui transgresse, sans équivoque, les conventions esthétiques établies, est Majida Khattari. Sortie de l'Ecole des Beaux-Arts en 1995, cette jeune Marocaine travaille à Paris où elle a organisé, en 2001, des défilés de mode, hautement politisés.[16] Pour *Veil*, elle expose, sur un petit poste de télévision, un vidéo-montage composé de séquences filmées de ses défilés, intercalées de pages de texte en arabe. Je me propose d'analyser la *Performance No. 2* qui est divisée en deux parties. La première est intitulée 'Le Pouvoir' : c'est un défilé d'hommes perruqués à la Louis XIV, vêtus comme des femmes du XVIIè siècle de robes en tissus somptueux et colorés flottant sur des crinolines. Dans la deuxième : 'Les mille et une souffrances du tchadori', on observe des mannequins femmes habillées d'un vêtement-voile-peau noir, souvent près du corps qui laisse parfois la tête et les épaules dégagées. Les acteurs et actrices de cette *Performance No. 2* ont en commun une marche/démarche difficile qui les ramène, après une exposition éphémère, vers l'anonymat sombre des coulisses.

Attachant beaucoup d'attention aux détails, Khattari s'est appliquée à dupliquer le défilé de haute-couture parisien classique : *catwalk* violemment éclairé, spectateurs assis de chaque côté, grande ligne droite menant à une plate-forme sur laquelle les mannequins effectuent un tournant, avant de remonter enfin vers les coulisses, le tout en musique. Dans l'enregistrement vidéo du spectacle, la caméra (et donc notre œil) ne possède que deux plans : l'un voyant la progression des modèles se rapprochant petit à petit de nous et l'autre les observant de dos lorsqu'ils/elles effectuaient leur virage avant la remontée finale. Toutes les conventions esthétiques du genre sont respectées par Khattari : des mannequins beaux et élancés apparaissent sous les éclairages, défilent lentement vers nous, tournent et se croisent, dans un ballet minutieusement orchestré depuis les coulisses.

Le respect des conventions s'arrête là. Il s'agit, on l'a compris, d'un exercice d'ironie pure qui ridiculise, du grand siècle à nos jours, l'auto-perception de gloire et de grandeur historique et politique (Louis XIV et sa dictature de droit divin) et de prestige économique et esthétique (l'industrie des produits de luxe et la haute-couture) dont se leurrent les Français de toutes les époques. L'ordre masculin exhibé est à la fois magistral, dans sa mise en scène, et comique, par l'anachronisme d'accoutrements inadéquats. Mais, si la chamade des larges crinolines du patriarcat et de la dictature, qui défilent en couple et se heurtent les unes aux autres, prête à sourire, l'exhibition des restrictions physiques qu'impose le voile musulman sur le corps féminin est beaucoup plus douloureuse. Les corps des modèles femmes symbolisent alors l'impossiblité d'actions vitales : voir, parler, aller, faire et être. Ainsi le voile couvre complètement un visage aveuglé et muet, ainsi le corps voilé serré se traîne à genoux au lieu de marcher, ainsi les mains restreintes par des attaches aux poignets se trouvent paralysées, ainsi la vie s'arrête avec le souffle compressé à la taille par une large ceinture. Tous les accessoires, camisoles de force, épingles, bijoux, font soit entrave, soit violence au corps. Quant au maquillage, il renforce la détresse. On peut juger la performance de Khattari très occidentalisée mais, elle a néanmoins le courage de représenter ce que d'autres considèrent encore comme irreprésentable[17] et l'ambition de s'attaquer au rêve occidental et patriarcal de souveraineté.[18]

L'expérience 'du sujet regardé'[19] ou de celle[20] qui est photographiée derrière le voile

Dans *La Chambre claire*, Roland Barthes ne consacre qu'une dizaine de pages au point de vue du sujet regardé.[21] Exception faite du bruit du déclic de l'appareil : 'la seule chose que je supporte, que j'aime, qui me soit familière'[22], cette expérience-là, à savoir le portrait de soi (de lui) se regardant 'sur un papier', équivaut globalement à une position inconfortable.[23] Barthes insiste sur l'artifice que constitue l'attitude du sujet posant pour l'objectif ainsi que sur la dépendance du sujet-objet.[24] L'impuissance de ce dernier face à la manipulation du photographe et à l'instantanéité du moment, qui va disparaître à jamais, est à lire dans une expérience de l'entre-deux qui va de la vie à la mort séparée par l'instant du déclic : '[...] je ne suis ni un sujet ni un objet, mais plutôt un sujet qui se sent devenir objet : je vis alors une micro-expérience de la mort (de la parenthèse); je deviens vraiment spectre.' (p. 30). Il analyse les 'forces' en présence comme la somme de quatre 'imaginaires'[25] qui correspondent aux intentions identitaires et esthétiques, projetées et combinées, du sujet-objet photographié et du photographe : 'Devant l'objectif, je suis à la fois : celui que je me crois, celui que je voudrais qu'on me croie, celui que le photographe me croit, et celui dont il se sert pour exhiber son art.' (p. 29).

A propos de ce bref point de vue, dont la nature extraordinairement subjective, une photo de sa mère enfant, ne sera entièrement dévoilée que très tardivement par Barthes[26], Jane Gallop note que quarante-trois chapitres au total sont consacrés dans *La Chambre claire,* à la lecture de l'image par une tierce partie spectatrice, ce qui lui fait dire que : '[...] almost all the rest of the writing on photography is surely from the perspective of what [Barthes] calls the "spectator" [...]. Formal discourse on photography is rarely from the standpoint of the photographed subject'.[27] Ce qui suit, dans cet article, est assurément un exercice difficile puisqu'il se propose d'explorer, sans sentimentalité ou occidentalisme exacerbés, la position de la femme maghrébine sujet. Il s'agira principalement de considérer le double statut du voile comme marque des domaines sexuel (*gender*) et émotionnel et comme vêtement signe d'appartenance à la tradition musulmane et au *gender* féminin.

Traditionnellement, au Maghreb, le voile connu dès la petite enfance est un voile de la domesticité qui est architectural, c'est le *mashrabiyya*.[28] En bois sculpté, cet écran, qui fait office de mur dans les maisons, est une ligne de démarcation autant physique que sexuelle. Il délimite les espaces privé et publique, clôt le domaine privé des femmes et en interdit l'accès aux hommes (et aux photographes). Bailey et Tawadros insistent : l'écran en question n'est pas le mur de la prison car l'air, la lumière, le regard et la communication verbale passent et sont donc permis dans ce que ces auteurs appellent : 'a dynamic practice in which both men and women are implicated' qui fait du voilement une *gendered* praxis ni unidirectionnelle ni fixe.[29] Pour eux, la vie existe bien des deux côtés du rideau de bois, dans la rue comme dans les appartements privés des Maghrébines.[30] Ici, les *slits* architecturaux (mot traduit, jusqu'à la douleur, par mon dictionnaire en : fente, incision, déchirure) sont donc bien des lieux de passage et de communication.[31]

Aujourd'hui, la fente du voile-vêtement islamiste est devenue expressive et réflexive, et la photographie et les arts visuels, surtout la production appartenant à des artistes femmes, s'appliquent enfin à la représenter comme tel. A l'exposition *Veil*, la projection vidéo autobiographique de l'artiste d'origine algérienne Zineb Sedira, *Silent Sight* (2000), dure une douzaine de minutes.[32] Dans un bandeau rectangulaire projeté à hauteur d'homme/de femme, deux yeux maquillés au khôl noir et encadrés du voile blanc de l'écran nous fixent, clignent des paupières et bougent. Le voile se dissout dans le fondu blanc de l'écran de projection et avec lui, l'aveuglement colonial. Ce regard de femme-là exprime, avant tout, l'assurance, la confiance et le contrôle; ce qu'il suggère/encourage, c'est, pour la femme voilée, d'être vue et lue. La voix-off sur la vidéo dit et parfois chuchotte, en anglais, un commentaire-témoignage d'enfant de mère voilée : 'I remember...'. Le voile y est central mais nommé par un 'it' neutre. Quant au discours, il est articulé sur un narratif en trois temps, avec des phrases qui contiennent ou commencent par : 'sometimes', 'perhaps' et 'most of the time'. Les premières expriment des angoisses infantiles liant l'anonymat de la mère à la peur de la perte de celle-ci chez la fille : 'the anxiety of confusing her with someone else was sometimes so strong' et 'I would be scared of losing her'. Les secondes posent des questions sans espoir de réponses : '[perhaps] she just accepted it' ou 'she felt protected by it'. Enfin, les dernières se veulent positivement rassurantes pour la fille devenue adulte: '[most of the time] love her for who she was'.

Le voile de Sedira n'est donc pas à lire seulement comme un code physique opaque aux limites bien déterminées mais aussi comme un voile mental, perméable et transparent, parce que prêt à traduire, de façon subjective, des directions multiples et parfois contradictoires imposées par des traditions ou idéologies d'avant, pendant et d'après la colonisation. Pour la femme musulmane, si le voile islamique est traditionnellement un signe extérieur de maturité qui protège autant que rassure, que faire de sa tradition dans une époque postcoloniale ? Comment, pour l'artiste, représenter à la fois la visibilité et l'invisibilité de ce voile, qui veut transgresser les interdits, les stéréotypes et paradigmes culturels existants ? On trouve, certes, au centre du message de Zineb Sedira, le dilemme d'une Beur de la première génération en situation de conflit identitaire à cause de sa géographie personnelle postcoloniale.[33] Mais, il faut insister, si cette division basée sur le *gender* existait dans la tradition, le conflit entre la femme musulmane et son corps a bien été introduit par et avec la pénétration colonialiste. A la base de tous les exercices de mémoire des artistes femmes exposant pour *Veil*, il y a la nécessité de déconstruire le colonialisme et la volonté de marquer collectivement l'engagement, forcé ou volontaire, de leur culture maternelle avec l'idéologie et l'économie occidentales dominantes, en tant que processus irréversible, qui a transformé irrémédiablement la signification du voile aux niveaux local et international, pour des générations de femmes. Dans la période actuelle, le voile mental d'un orientalisme, qui ne voit que le symbole de la répression et/ou de la résistance à son ordre moral, sociétal et sexuel, présente un obstacle à ne pas sous-estimer: 'Let's not pass too quickly over the tenacity of the veil. For the Western gaze, the veil and the Orient are so closely entwined', dit Sedira.[34] Dans un effort de construction identitaire multiculturelle, son projet artistique accédera et fera partager un espace émotionnel privé et public, culturel et social, politique et sexuel dans lequel : 'The unveiled woman is seen as an individual and civilised subject, a far cry from the over-represented and culturally constructed veiled woman, who is considered anonymous, passive and exotic'.[35] Comme pour Barthes, le point d'attache ou d'ancrage, la gachette ou le déclic (*catch release mechanism*) de cette démarche passe par une identification avec la mère, à travers le regard photographié.

Lectures de photographies de femmes dévoilées : origines, éclairages et résistances
Si, à quelques exceptions près[36], et grâce particulièrement à Roland Barthes historien de l'art et critique avant d'être fils dans *La Chambre claire*, on accepte aujourd'hui implicitement qu'il n'y ait pas d'images sans lecture de l'image, il reste à préciser ce que constitue l'origine des rhétoriques discursives dans les arts visuel et plastique, le travail idéologique qu'elles opèrent ainsi que la résistance du discours analytique à reproduire/refléter ce processus idéologique. J'illustrerai mon propos de deux portraits d'Algériennes dévoilées de 1960 pris par le photographe, Marc Garanger, alors appelé du contingent. Pour les autorités françaises d'occupation, il dut, en une dizaine de jours, prendre pratiquement deux mille photos de femmes dévoilées sur ordre du commandant de garnison ;

ces clichés étaient destinés à la constitution de cartes d'identité en vue de la naturalisation (française) de ces autochtones.

Aujourd'hui, toute lecture occidentale de la mise en scène que constitue une photo trouve ses racines dans un double héritage culturel, grec et romain, qui oppose perceptions et conceptions du naturel et rend difficile la symbiose entre l'esthétique et l'éthique, dans l'analyse de l'image.

Comme nous le rappelle Serge Tisseron, pour les Grecs, l'image, *eikôn*, était un vaste concept au sein duquel le concept de ressemblance/vraisemblance, *omoiôsis*, n'était pas systématiquement présent.[37] Dans la représentation des corps, l'art consistait à transcender le niveau de la fragmentation du Beau dans la nature, pour atteindre, à travers la création, une œuvre d'art unie dans l'espace, qui privilégiait le rapport des corps et leur organisation. Ainsi, appliquée au portrait photo de femme-sujet-unique et dans une logique qui ne met pas en valeur la vraisemblance, le discours sur l'image tend à privilégier des considérations esthétiques, de l'ordre de la composition dans les limites du cadre (position du personnage, son interaction avec le décor), voire à refléter une absence de flexibilité de construction de la photographie par rapport à la peinture.[38]

En 1960, dans l'Algérie alors occupée par l'armée française, la première lecture (après celle du photographe, j'y reviendrai) des photos d'Algériennes dévoilées de Marc Garanger fut une lecture 'esthétique'. C'est le photographe qui le confirme:

> La première exposition de ces photographies a eu lieu à la fin de l'année 1960, quand j'ai aligné les photos d'identité, tirées en 4 x 4 cm, agrafées en six exemplaires, sur le bureau du capitaine, à Aumale (maintenant Sour El Ghozlane), quelques jours après la première série de prises de vue. Le capitaine, en découvrant les photographies, a ameuté les officiers de l'état-major en poussant des cris : 'Venez voir, venez voir comme elles sont laides ! Venez voir ces macaques, on dirait des singes!'[39]

Les officiers (on peut supposer qu'ils ont eu la même réaction que leur capitaine) ne lisent dans ces portraits que la banalité à deux niveaux : le sujet féminin, s'il est central dans le cliché, n'est en rien unique puisqu'il est multiplié des milliers de fois et le décor est sans intérêt puisqu'il ne s'agit toujours que des murs blanchis d'une *mechta* ordinaire [Pl. IV]. En revanche, ils perçoivent, avec une grande excitation, la laideur de cette féminité-spectacle. A partir de la mise en scène d'images instiguée par le photographe, comment déchiffrer, aujourd'hui, le 'rebus' de cette féminité-là ?[40] Comment lire la topographie fantasmatique du corps féminin dévoilé perçu comme abject ? L'analyse des procédés de codification, signes et canons, imposés individuellement et collectivement, par le colonialisme, offre quelques réponses. Dans le contexte politique de 1960, tout justifie la violence de l'acte (le dévoilement) et la violence politique et sexuelle (la colonisation). Ainsi, le registre de lecture correspond à un index/lexique qui dévalorise clairement les données présentes sur l'image observée. Esthétiquement, les signes visuels de l'abject sont : une femme échevelée, très/trop maquillée, au visage tatoué et portant des bijoux ostentatoires. Le référent est à l'exact opposé. En Europe, avant de poser pour une photo d'identié, une femme (ou un homme d'ailleurs) use toute une stratégie qui tend à embellir ou corriger le naturel. Quant au voyeurisme encouragé par le capitaine, il trouve, dans la laideur invoquée, suffisamment de matière ou de chair exposée et de regards méprisants, soumis ou ambivalents de victimes impuissantes, pour renforcer toute perversion sado-masochiste existant déjà chez ces militaires colons [Pl. V]. L'anonymat, aussi, a un rôle à jouer; ces Algériennes dévoilées vont devenir un groupe d'indigènes noires, barbares et violables en masse : 'ces macaques', dans le vocabulaire du capitaine. La définition du fétichisme que propose Laura Mulvey : 'a psychological and social structure that disavowed knowledge in favour of belief' s'apparente dangereusement ici à celle du racisme.[41] Dans la psyché des colons et l'ordre sociétal colonial, le *knowledge* est la valeur identitaire, religieuse, socio-culturelle et sexuelle du hijab et la nature des femmes algériennes qui sont ici violées; le *belief* est le statut inférieur d'objet ou de marchandise du voile et de la femme indigène à qui on 'offre' l'accès à la supériorité par la nationalité française, une sorte de rédemption religieuse, sexuelle et sociale.[42]

    J'en viens à la lecture 'latine' de Marc Garanger. Pour les Romains, au contraire des Grecs, l'image était soumise au concept plus fort de la ressemblance, *similitudo*; l'image y était toujours une ressemblance/vraisemblance exprimée. En cela, une lecture 'latine' appartient à un arrêt sur l'événement, qui fige l'instant/le temps et suggère des états antérieur et postérieur séparés par le moment du déclic.

Cette explication correspond à la lecture politique et historique de Garanger, photographe engagé. Il connaît le rêve colonialiste français en Algérie et la réalité de 'la guerre sans nom' avant d'être appelé au front, s'y oppose et voit, dans la commission de ces photos, un moyen d'action à long terme, contre la dynamique de destruction de la société algérienne.[43] Ce qu'il dit dans le document manuscrit, qui sert de préface à la dernière édition d'une sélection de ses photos [Pl. VI], c'est, qu'au moment du déclic et à travers le regard de ces Algériennes dévoilées de force, il reçoit la *hogra*, l'humiliation, d'un double viol défini par Frantz Fanon : 'Thus the rape of the Algerian woman in the dream of a European is always preceded by a rending of the veil. We here witness a double deflowering. Likewise, the woman's conduct is never one of consent or acceptance, but of abject humility'.[44]

Le premier grand mérite de Marc Garanger reste sa lecture immédiatement historique de la symbolique du voile et du regard : humiliation, soumission mais aussi résistance, confrontation ; son talent est d'être parvenu à changer l'usage public identitaire originaire et, par là même, à transformer la mémoire collective française future.[45]

Reste à expliquer l'endurance du discours sur la photographie et le visuel à ne pas produire la synthèse entre esthétique et politique. Laura Wexter analyse le poids de la tradition grecque sur l'actuel discours critique sur les arts visuels non seulement comme l'origine du refus du discours à accéder au politique, mais encore comme un acte idéologique délibéré, qu'elle nomme *anekphrasis* (*ekphrasis* étant l'art et le talent de mettre des mots sur des images) et définit comme : 'an active and selective refusal to read photography - its graphic labor, its social space - even when one is busy textualizing and contextualizing all other kinds of cultural documents'.[46] Elle fait, enfin, de ce potentiel dangereusement ignoré, une forme de racisme et de sexisme institutionalisés : 'The comparative neglect of critical attention to the raced, classed, and gendered productions of the photographic image is a form of cultural resistance. It represses the antidemocratic potential of photography'.[47] Comme aux origines de la photographie, la résistance actuelle à lire un message politique correspond à une pratique de la représentation et à une orchestration d'un regard à sens unique extrêmement politisées et développées, par un ordre social bourgeois cherchant à asseoir son pouvoir politique. La photographie, parce qu'elle stimule le principe du *simulitudo,* vraisemblance et vérité, sur la base d'un naturel et d'une nature présentés comme ils existent dans la réalité, constitue : un moyen idéal de contrôle de la représentation, un véhicule idéologique privilégié et un outil d'exclusion sans faille. D'où, à mon avis, l'extrême nécessité d'une action concertée et engagée en matière de critique théorique, qui conduirait à faire des parallèles, voire des amalgames, entre des domaines critiques souvent isolés : race, classes, *gender* et sexualité.

La photographie est donc bien une pratique privée limitée, à valeur de pratique sociale, qui peut défier la mémoire collective établie. J'en donnerai pour exemple les photos de Marc Garanger dont le second grand mérite est d'avoir résisté aux tentations de retoucher esthétiquement ses clichés et le troisième d'avoir exposé ses portraits sur la scène politique quand la guerre était encore une réalité.[48]

Pour conclure, il me semble qu'on a multiplié, en un siècle, les fonctions et les symboles du voile : sexy et exotique, pour l'orientalisme des harems, des hammams et des théâtres parisiens, puisamment développé comme thème par une poétique qui va du texte littéraire au cinéma en passant par la photographie et, symbolique et stratégique, aujourd'hui plus que jamais, dans sa représentation et son interprétation politiques, multifonctionnelles, pluridisciplinaires et multiculturelles. Il resterait à préciser la spécificité du positionnement de la spectatrice en tant que sujet-femme et lectrice, et à insister, sur l'attrait puissant, *gender* et sexualité confondus, du mystère de nos origines quand il s'agit de 'gazing into the womb'.[49]

Pl. 1 :
©Musée de l'Homme – Paris
Fonds Clérambault

Pl. 2 :
©Musée de l'Homme – Paris
Fonds Clérambault

Pl. 3 :
©Musée de l'Homme – Paris
Fonds Clérambault

Pl. 4 :
Collection privée du photographe

Pl. 5 :
Collection privée du photographe

En 1960, je faisais mon service militaire en Algérie.

L'armée française avait décidé que les autochtones devaient avoir une carte d'identité française pour mieux contrôler leurs déplacements dans les " villages de regroupement ".

Comme il n'y avait pas de photographe civil, on me demanda de photographier tous les gens des villages avoisinants : Aïn Terzine, Bordj Okhriss, le Merdour, le Meghnine, Souk el Khrémis.

J'ai ainsi photographié près de 2000 personnes, en grande majorité des femmes, à la cadence de 200 par jour.

Dans chaque village, les populations étaient convoquées par le chef de poste. C'est le visage des femmes qui m'a beaucoup impressionné. Elles n'avaient pas le choix. Elles étaient dans l'obligation de se dévoiler et de se laisser photographier. Elles devaient s'asseoir sur un tabouret, en plein air, devant le mur blanc d'une mechta.

J'ai reçu leur regard à bout portant, premier témoin de leur protestation muette, violente.

Je veux leur rendre témoignage.

Marc Garanger

Pl. 6 :
© Marc Garanger

NOTES

---

[1] Susan Sontag, On Photography (Penguin Books, 1977), p. 69 : 'Photographs are, of course, artifacts. But their appeal is that they also seem, in a world littered with photographic relics, to have the status of found objects -unpremeditated slices of the world. Thus, they trade simultaneously on the prestige of art and the magic of the real. They are clouds of fantasy and pellets of information'. Voir aussi Roland Barthes, 'L'effet de réel', in Littérature et réalité (Points Seuil, 1982).

[2] David A. Bailey et Gilane Tawadros, co-éditeurs du catalogue de l'exposition Veil, définissent l'orientalisme comme: 'a system of knowledge and belief, a structure by which Europe illustrates its cultural and political superiority over the Orient', 'Introduction', in Veil, Veiling, Representation and Contemporary Art, Catalogue de l'exposition Veil (inIVA, 2003), p. 18.

[3] Cette exposition internationale se trouvait à The New Art Gallery, Walsall, au printemps 2003.

[4] Voir Diana R. Blank 'A Veil of Controversy : the Construction of a Tchador Affair in the French Press', in 'Interventions', International Journal of Postcolonial Studies, Vol. 1, No. 4 (Routledge, 1999).

[5] Les études sur l'orientalisme et le postorientalisme étant très nombreuses, voir les ouvrages de Edward Said et Frantz Fanon et pour l'impact du mythe sur les figures de la sexualité féminine à la fin de siècle, Elaine Showalter, 'The Veiled Woman' in Sexual Anarchy (Bloomsbury, 1991), pp. 144-68.

[6] Roland Barthes, La Chambre claire (Le Seuil, 1980), p. 22. Mon texte de référence.

[7] Barthes, La Chambre claire, p. 22 : 'L'Operator, c'est le photographe'.

[8] Réunies lors de la conférence Family Pictures/Shapes of Memory (Dartmouth College, 1996), des féministes de renom ont utilisé la subjectivité de Barthes comme point de départ à une démarche qui 'open up the familial gaze to new forms of intimate engagement in a public forum', ed. Marianne Hirsch, The Familial Gaze (University Press of New England, 1999), p. 346. Je souligne ces termes péjoratifs qui évoquent : le 'trou de la serrure', un Peeping Tom, et 'la cohorte', une foule anonyme et sans intérêt.

[9] Il fut longtemps expert médico-légal à la préfecture de police de Paris. Pour ses diagnostiques, il utilisait des méthodes visuelles qui comprenaient l'analyse des vêtements, mimiques, attitudes et autres gestes à la limite du perceptible. Il s'intéressait plus particulièrement à l'automatisme mental et à l'érotomanie : 'l'illusion délirante d'être aimé par quelqu'un' (Le Petit Larousse Illustré 2000). Jacques Lacan fut interne dans le service du docteur Clérambault.

[10] Ces photographies sont conservées, aujourd'hui, au Musée de l'Homme, à Paris. Les archives comportent également un certain nombre d'articles écrits par Clérambault à l'occasion de trois conférences sur les drappés indigènes et arabes, entre 1921 et 1928, et un congrès d'anthropologie, en 1931.

[11] Jananne Al-Ani, Catalogue de Veil, p. 103.

[12] Serge Tisseron, Le Mystère de la chambre claire, Psychologie et inconscient (Champs Flammarion, 1996), pp. 105-06.

[13] Tisseron, Le Mystère, p. 103.

[14] Tisseron, *Le Mystère*, p. 106. Il se réfère ici, bien entendu, au stade du miroir de Lacan. Je note que le point de vulnérabilité psychique et l'affect mis en évidence chez le photographe et le spectateur, se rapprochent extraordinairement de ceux observés, par Walter Benjamin, chez les premiers sujets photographiés, au XIXè siècle : 'What was inevitably found inhuman, one might even say deadly, in daguerrotype was the prolonged looking into the camera, since the camera records one's likeness without returning one's gaze. But looking at someone carries the implicit expectation that our look will be returned by the person to whom it is directed', Walter Benjamin, 'On Some Motifs in Baudelaire', in *Illuminations*, ed. Hannah Arendt (Jonathan Cape, 1970), pp. 189-90, texte original de 1939 : 'Über einige Motive bei Baudelaire', *Zeitschrift für Sozialforschung*, VIII, 1-2.

[15] Laura Mulvey, *Fetishism and Curiosity* (Indiana University Press, 1996), p. 14. Le 17 novembre 1934, Clérambault mit en scène sa propre mort : assis dans un fauteuil, face à un miroir, il se tira un coup de révolver dans la bouche.

[16] Au printemps 2001, au Centre Georges Pompidou. Elle est exposée à la Tate Gallery, Liverpool.

[17] Un environnement qui, non seulement valorise la soumission féminine et la supériorité masculine mais encore, fait barrage aux jeunes musulmanes instruites qui aspirent à une vie professionnelle active.

[18] Voir Kaja Silverman à propos de J-L Godard : 'For the author of *Histoire(s) du cinéma*, [...] the dream that extends uninterruptedly from the nineteenth to the twentieth century is sovereignty', 'The Dream of the Nineteenth Century', *Camera Obscura 51*, Vol. 17, No. 3 (Duke University Press, 2002), p. 7.

[19] Barthes, *La Chambre claire*, p. 24: 'Je n'avais à ma disposition que deux expériences : celle du sujet regardé et celle du sujet regardant'.

[20] Barthes, *La Chambre claire*, p. 22 : ' Et celui ou cela qui est photographié, c'est la cible, le référant [...]'. Je mets le pronom démonstratif au féminin.

[21] Barthes, *La Chambre claire*, pp. 24-33.

[22] Barthes, *La Chambre claire*, p. 32.

[23] Barthes, *La Chambre claire*, p. 28.

[24] Barthes, *La Chambre claire*, p. 25 : '[...] je me constitue en train de "poser", je me fabrique instantanément un autre corps, je me métamorphose à l'avance en image. Cette transformation est active : je sens que la Photographie crée mon corps ou le mortifie, selon son bon plaisir [...]..'.

[25] Barthes, *La Chambre claire*, p. 29.

[26] Voir Jane Gallop, 'Observations of a Mother', in *The Familial Gaze*, p. 79.

[27] Gallop, 'Observations of a Mother', p. 67.

[28] En Europe, un des exemples les plus élaborés et mécanisés de *mashrabiyya* est celui de la façade sud de l'Institut du monde arabe, à Paris.

[29] Bailey et Tawadros, Catalogue de *Veil*, p. 23.

[30] Pour une lecture socio-historique de la vie du côté intérieur des *mashrabiyyas*, voir Assia Djebar, *Femmes d'Alger dans leur appartement* (Des femmes, 1980).

[31] En argot anglais, *the slit* est aussi *the cunt*.

[32] Zineb Sedira étudia à la Slade School of Art et au Royal College of Arts ; elle vit et travaille à Londres. Pour 2003-4, elle prépare une exposition en solo à la Cornerhouse, Manchester.

[33] Elevée et éduquée à Paris, dans les années 60 et 70, elle a aussi grandi au sein d'une communauté arabe musulmane.

[34] Sedira, Catalogue de *Veil*, p. 70.

[35] Sedira, Catalogue de *Veil*, p. 70.

[36] Des exceptions seraient, par exemple, dans la photographie traditionnelle, les rouleaux de pellicules qui ne sont jamais développés, et dans la photographie digitale, l'option de suppression presque simultanée à la prise de vue qui demeure irréversible une fois l'image effacée.

[37] Tisseron, p. 50.

[38] Le photo-montage serait ici une technique palliative qui prouverait que le/la photographe peut aussi construire une œuvre à partir de la fragmentation des corps. Voir, par exemple, *Black Christ* de la photographe américaine d'origine jamaïcaine, Renée Cox.

[39] Marc Garanger, *Femmes Algériennes 1960* (Altantica, 2002), p. 121. Il s'agit de la troisième publication; deux autres sélections de photos avaient déjà été publiées chez Contrejour, en 1982 et 1989.

[40] Le mot est emprunté à Laura Mulvey, p. xii.

[41] Mulvey, p. xi.

[42] Voir Franck Fanon: 'The occupying forces, in applying their maximum psychological attention to the veil worn by Algerian women, were obviously bound to achieve some results. Here and there it thus happened that a woman was 'saved', and symbolically unveiled.', 'Algeria Unveiled', in *Studies in a Dying Colonialism* (Earthscan, 1989), p. 38.

[43] Titre du film documentaire de Patrick Rotman et Bertrand Tavernier de 1992. Pour un témoignage d'Algérienne sur la torture, le premier en quarante ans selon *Le Monde* du 15 juin 2001, voir Louisette Ighilahriz, *Algérienne* (Fayard-Calmann-Lévy, 2001).

[44] Frantz Fanon. Cité par le catalogue de *Veil*, p. 77. Edition originale en français de 1959, *L'An cinq de la Révolution*.

[45] Voir le pseudo-documentaire de Gillo Pontecorvo, *La Bataille d'Alger* (1965) où l'on montre que le haïk permit aux militantes du FLN de cacher armes et bombes et de passer ainsi les barrages militaires.

[46] Laura Wexler, 'Seeing Sentiment', in *The Familial Gaze*, p. 251.

[47] Wexler, 'Seeing Sentiment', p. 251.

[48] Dès 1961, des photographies sont parues dans *l'Illustré* suisse, avec un texte de Charles-Henri Favrot qui dénonçait cette guerre.

[49] David Lodge, *Small World* (Secker & Warburg, 1984), pp. 26-27. Cité par Elaine Showalter, p. 166.

The Forbidden Real of French Filmic Testimony

Libby Saxton
University of Cambridge

In the provocative essay which opens his recent volume *Welcome to the Desert of the Real*, Slavoj Žižek offers an analysis of the televisual *mise-en-scène*, or staging, of the attack on the World Trade Centre.[1] Diagnosing a twentieth-century 'passion for the Real', a longing for the unmediated experience of the ever elusive (Lacanian) Real of trauma, death and material decay, the thinker inverts the more common reading of the events of September 11th 2001 as an eruption of the Real of catastrophe into an image-saturated society. For Žižek, it is not the Real that intrudes as desired but its spectacular other: an 'image', 'semblance', 'spectre' or 'effect'. (That the target selected for the attack should be the symbolic centre of 'virtual' capitalism, of economic speculation divorced from its origins in material production, adds weight to his argument.) The desire to reclaim the Real that haunts a digitalized capitalist First World where 'real life' itself has been 'de-materialized', reversed into a 'spectral show' (Žižek reads the Wachowski brothers' *Matrix* (1999) and Peter Weir's *The Truman Show* (1998) as intriguing enactments of this condition) can thus be seen to entail a fundamental paradox: 'the "passion for the Real" culminates in its apparent opposite, in a *theatrical spectacle*, [...] in the pure semblance of the spectacular *effects of the Real*' (9–10). Ironically, thus frustrated, our longing for the Real returns us once more to the image, in search of a substitute, in search of 'the thrill of the Real as the ultimate "effect" [...] from digitalized special effects, through reality TV and amateur pornography, up to snuff movies' (12).

In the Žižekian 'desert of the Real', it is thus only the real itself that remains forbidden. As it enters a realm of pure representation, where images stolen from reality are drained of meaning and referential power by endless televisual looping, the real of mass trauma is rendered inaccessible, even invisible. My subject, then, is this forbidden real, more specifically, the related possibility that there are certain realities that prohibit representation. In this context, Žižek's reflections offer an uncomfortable but germane point of departure. The reference to snuff pornography in the quotation above is sickening, but telling, for in the snuff movie, which Žižek proposes as the 'ultimate truth' of virtual reality, real pain and real death are not only spectacularized, but also re-eroticized. Thus a parallel emerges between the snuff genre and media images of the terrorist attack, libidinally reinvested, in Žižekian discourse, as the object of a collective American fantasy (witness Hollywood's taste for apocalyptic scenarios). Desiring a real that remains forbidden, we seek refuge instead in images, in the very de-realization of death and trauma.

Yet in the Žižekian dialectic of spectacle and Real, it is the testimonial capacity of the image – its capacity to bear truthful witness to history – that is the first casualty. At a time when new technologies of visual representation are transforming our relationship to history by bringing it to unprecedented visibility as pure media spectacle (cameras attached to falling bombs in the first Gulf War and 'embedded' journalists in the most recent one are cases in point), paradoxically, the real seems to be retreating further into invisibility. Jean-Louis Comolli warns us of this risk when, targeting 'l'assaut donné à la réalité elle-même par la fabrication d'un spectacle plus réaliste qu'elle', he argues that the 'monde spectaculaire' 'triomphe de tous ses référents' to become 'une source référentielle plus réelle que les autres'.[2] If reality is increasingly located in the spectacle itself, if the visible can no longer be equated with the real, then the image would appear to have forsaken its relationship with history, its capacity to bear witness.

I use 'bearing witness' here and in what follows in the specific sense of an act predicated upon an ethical relationship – as well as response (and responsibility) – to the real. To bear witness, or to testify ('testimony' is derived from the Latin 'testis', meaning 'witness') has legal connotations, but it is the ethical dimension of testimony I would like to explore here. Defined by Emmanuel Levinas as an 'opening of self' to otherness, bearing witness is not merely a performance but an intersubjective process that precipitates an encounter with alterity, not only with a listener but also with a real.[3] While the ethical injunction to bear witness that emerges from historical trauma is rooted in the legal injunction to attest the truth when it is called into question, when the real remains elusive, this ethical injunction is also irreducible to the more restricted demands of the law. In her seminal volume *Testimony*, Shoshana Felman argues that while the legal model of the trial dramatizes a 'crisis of evidence', testimony, once rethought outside this limiting, institutionalized model, entails a more radical epistemological and ethical 'crisis of truth'.[4] Whence the aporia of testimony identified by so many survivor-witnesses of historical traumas such as the Holocaust: in such contexts, the impossibility of silence (the ethical imperative to testify) coexists with an impossibility of testimony (the epistemological difficulties of giving a truthful account of the real of trauma).[5]

To speak of art, and more specifically the image, bearing witness, thus entails a privileging not only of its relationship to history, but also of its status as an ethical response to the real. Implicit in Žižek's analysis is the threat posed to this status when the image, corrupted by the spectacularizing tendencies of Hollywood and new media technologies, loses its bond with the real. This is a threat that has long preoccupied French filmmakers and theorists of cinema (an art that has frequently been associated with notions of the forbidden in representation, particularly with those forbidden pleasures that cast the spectator, in Gillian Rose's phrase, as 'the ultimate predator').[6] Exemplary is Jean-Luc Godard's persistent lament that cinema's documentary roots became diseased by the spectacular dictates of Eros and Thanatos ('a film is a girl and a gun'). In Godard's account, moreover, it was the historical trauma of Auschwitz that revealed the extent to which the moving image had distanced itself from the real. The director's frequently-rehearsed claim that cinema has failed to bear witness to the death camps looks highly problematic in the light of works such as Claude Lanzmann's *Shoah* (1985), but nevertheless sheds light on post-war discourses on the forbidden in art.[7] Paradigmatic of course is Adorno's radical (and later redefined) prohibition of poetry after Auschwitz, which famously addressed the possibility that certain realities are so traumatic that they must remain forbidden to representation on ethical grounds.

In reflecting on such discourses, certain French filmmakers have explored the potential of cinema to bear witness to traumatic realities in a way that resists the lure of spectacle, in order, precisely, to preserve certain realms of the real intact and inaccessible; in short, to bear witness to a forbidden real. Sensitive to the affinities between cinema and fascism, whose penchant for spectacular self-stagings has intrigued thinkers such as Gilles Deleuze, such filmmakers explore the possibility that while cinema has charted the triumph of the spectacular, it can also be a site of resistance to spectacularization, of a return to the real.[8] In particular, their works raise questions about representability in the context of extreme trauma, questions that have been refocused by recent debate on representation of the view through the spy-hole into the Nazi gas chambers.[9] This is a view that continues to haunt French film, and yet is forbidden on multiple grounds; in the face of the real of mass execution, the Jewish prohibition of images (*Bilderverbot*) reinforces the taboo on fiction controversially pronounced by Lanzmann, to identify a limit-point of cinematic ethics.

In what follows I would like to explore some of the ways French film and thought have interrogated and reconfigured such forbidden moments as testimonial encounters. Two of the most intriguing and consistent practitioners and theorists of the image as witness are the filmmaker Alain Resnais and the critic Serge Daney. Both share a belief in cinema's irreducibly ethical responsibility to the real, a belief formed in the aftermath of the trauma of the war, and in the present context they lend themselves to a parallel reading. Not only do Resnais's works, in particular his filmic reflection on the death camps, *Nuit et brouillard* (1955), occupy a unique place in Daney's thought (Nathalie Nezick identifies the early film as the critic's 'opus absolutum').[10] Director and theorist are also united on a deeper level in their identification of the cinematic image as a privileged medium for bearing witness. While I would suggest that Daney's location of an ethical core in the image cannot fully account for the testimonial power of Resnais's images, their capacity to evoke the real in all its unendurable horror, films such as *Nuit et brouillard* and *Muriel, ou le temps d'un retour* (1963) can help to clarify certain productive ellipses and tensions in Daney's argument. Reading Resnais and Daney against each other through the retrospective lens offered by Žižek will thus shed light on their location of the testimonial image, not only as the antidote to spectacle, but also as the condition for an ethical encounter with the forbidden real.

Where, then, does spectacle end and testimony begin? The gap between the image and the real that is implicit in Žižek's argument seems only to widen with advances in visual technologies, particularly – and paradoxically – when they appear to collapse this gap by offering images in real time. What was unprecedented about the images of September 11th was their immediacy; by the second plane crash we had become 'téléspectateurs témoins en temps réel'.[11] This eruption of real time into representation fuels contemporary concerns about the dissolution of the 'historical event'. As Vivian Sobchack puts it in her volume *The*

Persistence of History, 'event and its representation, immediacy and its mediation, have moved increasingly towards simultaneity. [...] Today, history seems to happen right now'.[12] Crucially, the simultaneity of reality and representation not only threatens the distinction between historical truth and fiction, rendering the real more elusive; it also eradicates the temporal gap that inhabits – and, for many contemporary trauma theorists, defines – traumatic experience.[13] This gap marks the temporal delay that splits the traumatic event from its psychic impact and defers its figuration as testimony (that belated or retroactive impact of trauma upon the survivor-witness that gives rise to the ambiguous Freudian concept of *Nachträglichkeit*). If such a gap is the first prerequisite for remembering and bearing witness, inevitably, then, its elision in the live spectacle would seem to threaten to render the image redundant as a vehicle for memory, mourning, and testimony.

This is surely one of the senses in which we should understand the often-cited Godardian thesis that television generates forgetting. Rendering the real as spectacle, contemporary media collude in the serial production of amnesia by erasing – rather than bearing witness to – historical trauma. The coverage of September 11th was symptomatic: the endless recycling of camcorder footage of the collapse of the towers drained an excess of visual witness of its testimonial meaning and status (whence the disturbing frequency of reports of viewers who thought they had simply tuned in to a disaster movie). At a time when the electronic spectacularization of suffering has become so ubiquitous that the real of death can only be apprehended as a fiction, surely a rethinking of the testimonial status of the moving image becomes imperative.

Daney's writings take this imperative as their point of orientation. For the critic, the cinematic image is defined, precisely, by its capacity to 'faire témoignage'.[14] Moreover, any attempt to elaborate an ethics of cinematic representation – an attempt which is at the core of his project – must be predicated on a dual recognition: that the moving image is a privileged medium for testimony to a traumatic real, and that there is something in this real that prohibits certain forms of the image. Indeed, his prose is shot through with a strong sense of the forbidden in representation; whence his use of formulations such as 'figures taboues' and 'montages interdits'.[15] In reflections infused with the Bazinian notion of the image as witness to history, Daney argues – interestingly, against Godard – that there are certain historical phenomena such as the Nazi death camps that, in a pre-televisual age, *only* cinema has seen or witnessed. Not only did the Nuremberg trials reveal the power of film as evidence; for Daney, it is cinema alone, unlike contemporary televisual spectacles, that is 'capable de camper aux limites d'une humanité dénaturée' (1994, 19). It is this unique position as witness that leads the writer to identify in the cinematic image a privileged bond with the real.

Daney explains this privilege, and the prohibitions that it entails, by means of a negative foil. For him, the zero point – the *a priori* – of cinematic ethics, 'l'axiome qui ne se discut[e] pas, le point limite de tout débat' (1994, 16), can be located in a single filmic moment, a moment that he returns to again and again in his writings, and that he refers to as 'le travelling de *Kapo*'. His allusion here is to a seminal critique of the spectacularization of suffering, Jacques Rivette's 'De l'abjection', an article that attacks a specific sequence in *Kapo* (1960), Gillo Pontecorvo's representation of Auschwitz, where a suicidal Emmanuelle Riva throws herself against the electrified barbed wire surrounding the camp.[16] What troubles Rivette is the way Pontecorvo's camera travels forward to reframe her lifeless body from a low angle, to create a more balanced, aesthetically-pleasing image. For Rivette, this reframing is abject because it aestheticizes and spectacularizes the body at the instant of death. In the death-ridden world of the camps, the fetishizing gaze of the classical narrative camera becomes unethical, even obscene: 'toute approche traditionnelle du « spectacle » [des camps] relève du voyeurisme et de la pornographie' (54).

As it filters through Rivette's critique into Daney, 'le travelling de *Kapo*' becomes not only a critical topos but also an ethical touchstone (even, he suspects in retrospective, a 'grigri protecteur' (1994, 30); significantly, Daney, like Adorno, later comes to modify his axiom). More specifically, Pontecorvo's 'travelling' comes to stand for what is forbidden in the image, as a form of cinephilic short-hand for the more nebulous and contested ethical prohibition articulated by thinkers such as Adorno. What Daney identifies as the 'necrophiliac' leanings of Pontecorvo's search for beauty inadvertently bring into sharp focus the ethical questions inherent (though so often elided) in all 'cinéma d'« après les camps »' (1994, 29). By privileging the aesthetic over the ethical, Pontecorvo's images move away from testimony towards spectacle and fiction, betraying their bond with the historical real. And for Daney (and this is where his analysis anticipates Žižek's psychoanalytic diagnosis), this is a bond that is increasingly under threat. For, in Daney's account, 'le travelling de *Kapo*' is a precursor to the 'spectacles électroniques' of contemporary warfare, as much as to the abject images of suffering that saturate our television screens.

However, where Daney's analysis departs from that of Žižek (as well as, notably, from those of Jean Baudrillard and Paul Virilio), is in its location of a site of resistance to the increasing dissolution of the real in representation. For Daney posits a crucial opposition between the televisual flux of images, a realm he calls *le visuel*, and *l'image*, which preserves a relationship with the real. The former is defined and irredeemably impoverished by its capacity to offer images from a single perspective only: '[...] *du point de vue du pouvoir*, c'est-à-dire d'un champ sans contrechamp (d'un champ qui annihile son contrechamp)'; '[au] visuel [...] il ne [...] manque rien, il est clos, en boucle, un peu à l'image du spectacle pornographique [...].'[17] Here, political critique meets ethical reflection: it is easier for the powerful to demonize and destroy a powerless other who is kept invisible, who is silenced and erased by television's metaphorical refusal of the reverse shot. But, for Daney, the homogenizing closure imposed, under the guise of complete transparency, on the real by *le visuel* finds a point of resistance in *l'image*. The latter is defined and inhabited, in contrast, by heterogeneity and lack, and is thus 'vouée à témoigner d'une certaine *altérité*': 'Qu'il y ait aussi *de l'autre* [...], c'est donc ça, l'image de cinéma. [...] Si l'image informait [...], ce n'était jamais du seul point de vue du plus fort, mais à partir d'un entre-deux où se dessinait, parfois *in extremis*, le visage du moins fort [...]' (1991, 193).

Unmistakable at such points in Daney is the residue of a Levinasian ethics derived from an original encounter with the face of the other, a face whose irreducible alterity and very vulnerability forbid violation.[18] Comolli has defined the power of cinema as its capacity to 'renvoyer les hommes les uns aux autres. Les renvoyer face à face' (22). As a self-acclaimed *ciné-fils*, Daney attributes his own 'adoption' of and by cinema to the same intuition, an intuition that cinema could teach him something that other art forms could not: 'à toucher inlassablement du regard à quelle distance de moi commence l'autre' (1994, 39). In response to the televisual erasure of the other's face (an erasure at the root of Godard's famous claim that television does not produce 'images' at all), Daney seems to be appealing for the search for a cinematicallymediated form of the Levinasian *face-à-face* (or, in the terms of the quotation above, 'un entre-deux').

However, the apparent cogency of such an appeal is undermined by a closer reading of Levinas's formulation of this encounter. Anticipating the misunderstandings to which his complex notion of *le visage* has indeed given rise, the philosopher's reflections on the *face-à-face* repeatedly emphasize that the face is never an object of vision or perception, that, on the contrary, it refuses visual appropriation. If, for Levinas, the face of the other is violated the moment it solidifies into a fixed image under the gaze of the self, then in fact the *face-à-face* would seem a singularly resistant model for a cinematic ethics. And indeed, this is the point at which an ellipsis appears to emerge in Daney's thought. For, parallel to the image's capacity to reveal the other's face, the critic posits an aporia: 'Si le visuel est une boucle, l'image est *à la fois un manque et un reste*' (1991, 194; my emphasis). Lack and residue, absence and excess: what Daney is identifying in the image are precisely the twin figures of the ineffable proper to the real of trauma. As such, they are also figures that point beyond the visible, beyond the simple revelation of the face of the other, to trouble the transparency of testimony. In the wake of Auschwitz, Daney argues, 'la sphère du visible a cessé d'être tout entière disponible: il y a des absences et des trous, des creux nécessaires et des pleins superflus, des images à jamais manquantes' (1994, 26). This irreducibility of the real of the camps to the visible would seem to cast fresh doubt upon the adequacy of the image as witness.

What are the implications of this tension in Daney's analysis for filmmakers? How might the face of the other be figured cinematically, not only as a revelation and residue, but also as a lack in the image, testimony to a real that must remain forbidden to representation? Writing on the inestimable impact on cinema of Allied footage of the death camps, Antoine de Baecque has reflected on some of the cinematic figures that might be available for such à project:

> Le cinéma moderne est né de ces images des camps, qui n'ont cessé de travailler en lui, de resurgir sous d'autres formes, regard-caméra, arrêt sur image, documentaire dans la fiction, flashback, montage, contemplation, malaise, ces figures spécifiquement cinématographiques qui témoignent de la présence obsessionnelle du palimpseste concentrationnaire.[19]

Almost all of these figures have been explored by Resnais, whose entire œuvre may be read as a testimony to this palimpsest, to the return of the real of the camps as a spectral absence-presence in the image. (Whence Gilles Deleuze's suggestion that all of Resnais's characters resemble camp survivors, those who return from the dead.) It is as an absence, a lack in the image, that the excesses of the real are figured by *Nuit et brouillard*. In contrast to Pontecorvo's 'travelling', Resnais's tracking shots here reveal only emptiness, unbodied spaces that create anxiety in the spectator. This is why, for Daney, the film epitomizes 'l'anti-spectacle' (1994, 23) (in the same vein, Henri Agel calls it 'l'anti-*Chien andalou*').[20] Under Resnais's lens, the present-day landscape of Auschwitz yields only traces of the horror that was. And if, in cinema, the trace, like the photographic image itself, points always to the absence of a real to which it constantly testifies, then we begin to see how Resnais's film sheds light on the tension in Daney's thinking. While every image of *Nuit et brouillard* inscribes its own inadequacy, its failure to testify in the face of such horror (an awareness that Jean Cayrol's commentary repeatedly struggles to articulate), it is precisely as they negate themselves, as they become what Daney calls 'non-images' (1994, 25), that they are able to confirm that 'ceci a eu lieu' (1999, 38), that they are able, in short, to bear witness.

The 'non-image' as a testimonial figure takes a more specific form in *Muriel*, a film that once again inscribes the possibility of its own failure to bear witness: 'Tu veux raconter Muriel. Mais Muriel ne se raconte pas' (the echoes of the *Scénario* of Resnais's earlier film, *Hiroshima mon amour* (1959), are telling: 'tout ce qu'on peut faire, c'est de parler de l'impossibilité de parler de Hiroshima').[21] In *Muriel*, the forbidden real is the experience of torture, that limit encounter that Jean Améry, reflecting on his own experiences at the hands of the Gestapo, discusses in Sadian terms as 'the radical negation of the other'.[22] It would seem apt, then, that the central encounter of the film takes the form of a *face-à-face*, and Resnais's staging of this encounter sheds intriguing light on Daney's argument. In a pivotal sequence, Bernard confesses to his role in the torture and beating to death of a woman he refers to as 'Muriel', a young Algerian resistance fighter. Specifically, he is haunted by a single memory-image of this experience, the moment when his victim suddenly returned his gaze: 'Son regard m'a fixé [...] Pourquoi moi?'. However, crucially, this is a *face-à-face* we never witness, for Bernard's testimony is accompanied not by images of Muriel's agonized look, but by anonymous home movie footage of his army life in Algeria. By substituting the (visible) banal for the (invisible) ineffable here, *Muriel* would seem to offer the 'non-image' in its purest form. Through the missing scenes, Resnais bears witness to the forbidden real as a lacuna at the heart of the image.

Like the traces of *Nuit et brouillard*, the invisible *face-à-face* of *Muriel* thus performs the testimonial function prescribed by Daney while refusing that appropriation of alterity proscribed by Levinas. In contrast to those of Pontecorvo, Resnais's images preserve the invisibility of the face of the other, its resistance to the spectator's gaze, and yet in the same gesture they bear witness to this face, as an absence, as radical alterity. It is in this testimonial capacity, then, that Resnais and Daney, read in tandem, locate the residually political and ethical core of the image, a capacity which is not without compelling contemporary implications, as I suggested at the outset of this piece. In an interview published in October 2001, Lanzmann and the *Cahiers du cinéma* critics posed the question 'il y a un après 11 septembre, pour le cinéma?'[23] If there is a future for cinema in the wake of such events, and, above all, in the wake of Auschwitz, the 'grand point aveugle de l'histoire du cinéma' (Nezick, 164), then surely it must lie in the search for images – and non-images – that mournfully inscribe this legacy, that bear witness while preserving the forbidden real intact. With uncomfortable prescience, Resnais and Daney alert us to the urgency of such a project.

NOTES

1 Slavoj Žižek, 'Passions of the Real, Passions of Semblance', in *Welcome to the Desert of the Real: Five Essays on September 11 and Related Dates* (Verso, 2002), pp. 5–32.
2 Jean-Louis Comolli and Jacques Rancière, *Arrêt sur histoire* (Éditions du Centre Pompidou, 1997), pp. 38, 43.
3 Emmanuel Levinas, 'Témoignage et éthique' (1976), in *Dieu, la mort et le temps* (Grasset, 1993), pp. 227–30 (p. 227). On the intersubjective structure of testimony, in particular the role of the listener, see Dori Laub, 'Bearing Witness, or the Vicissitudes of Listening', in Shoshana Felman and Laub, *Testimony: Crises of Witnessing in Literature, Psychoanalysis, and History* (Routledge, 1992), pp. 57–74.
4 Felman and Laub, *Testimony*, p. 7.

5 On this aporia of testimony, see, for example, Elie Wiesel and Jorge Semprun, *Se taire est impossible* (Mille et une Nuits / ARTE, 1995)

6 Gillian Rose, *Mourning Becomes the Law: Philosophy and Representation* (Cambridge University Press, 1996), p. 47.

7 Godard makes this claim, for example, in his monumental video essay *Histoire(s) du cinéma* (1988–1998).

8 Deleuze remarks, for example, that 'jusqu'au bout le nazisme se pense en concurrence avec Hollywood' (*Cinéma 2, L'Image-temps* (Minuit, 1985), p. 344).

9 This debate is at the core of the ongoing standoff between Godard and Lanzmann, and was reanimated by the photographic exhibition in Paris in 2001, 'Mémoire des camps'.

10 Nathalie Nezick, 'Le Travelling de *Kapo* ou le paradoxe de la morale', *Vertigo* 17 (1998) ('Lector in cinéma'), 160–4 (p. 163).

11 Charles Tesson, 'Retour à l'envoyeur', *Cahiers du cinéma* 561 (October 2001) ('Le Cinéma rattrapé par l'histoire'), 42–44 (p. 44).

12 *The Persistence of History: Cinema, Television, and the Modern Event*, ed. Vivian Sobchack (Routledge, 1996), p. 5.

13 In 'The Modernist Event', Hayden White offers an analysis of the way the disintegration of stable notions of the historical event undermines the concept of factuality (in *The Persistence of History*, ed. Sobchack, pp. 17–38 (p. 18)).

14 Daney, *Itinéraire d'un ciné-fils* (Jean-Michel Place, 1999), p. 38.

15 See, for example, Daney, 'Le travelling de *Kapo*', in *Persévérance* (Paris: POL, 1994), pp. 13–39 (p. 16).

16 Jacques Rivette, 'De l'abjection', *Cahiers du cinéma*, 120 (June 1961), 54–55.

17 Daney, *Devant la recrudescence des vols de sacs à main: cinéma, télévision, information* (Aléas Editeur, 1991), pp. 185, 192.

18 See, in particular, Levinas, *Totalité et infini: Essai sur l'exteriorité* (The Hague: Martinus Nijhoff, 1961) (especially 'Visage et éthique', pp. 168–95).

19 Antoine de Baecque, 'Premières images des camps: Quel cinéma après Auschwitz?', *Cahiers du cinéma* hors-série (November 2000) ('Le siècle du cinéma'), 62–66 (p. 66).

20 Henri Agel, *Miroir de l'insolite dans le cinéma français* (Cerf, coll. 'Septième Art', 1958), p. 170.

21 Marguerite Duras, *Hiroshima mon amour: scénario et dialogues* (Gallimard, 1960), p. 10.

22 Jean Améry, 'Torture', in *At the Mind's Limits: Contemplations by a Survivor on Auschwitz and its Realities* (Granta, 1999), pp. 21–40 (p. 35).

23 Lanzmann, 'Sur le courage', *Cahiers du cinéma* 561 (October 2001) ('Le Cinéma rattrapé par l'histoire'), 46–57 (p. 56).

'La Dernière étape des fédérés au Père-Lachaise': The Contribution of *Le Monde illustré* to the Right-Wing Myth of Paris and the Commune

Colette Wilson
Royal Holloway, University of London

This study will analyse the way that the so-called 'dernière étape des fédérés au Père-Lachaise' and the torching of Paris in the final week of the Commune were reported by the family-orientated and ostensibly non-political weekly journal, *Le Monde illustré*. In so doing, I will argue that, by drawing on the shared cultural heritage of its implied bourgeois readers, this journal (as part of the Paul Dalloz empire which also owned *Le Moniteur universel*, the government's quasi-official newspaper), was able to help lay the foundations of an alternative right-wing version of events which sought to censor, marginalize, and ultimately banish the Commune to the realm of the forbidden.[1] To date there has been no detailed analysis of the contribution made by *Le Monde illustré*, or indeed any other French illustrated journal, to anti-Communard discourse.[2]

Much has been written about the Commune from a number of perspectives (historical, political, social, feminist, literary, artistic), but it may prove helpful to preface this short study with a brief summary of the events which form the background to the articles and illustrations to be discussed.[3] The Commune was not an organized revolution but came about partly as the result of a number of unresolved social and political grievances dating back to the days of the Second Empire, and partly as a reaction by many Parisians to the humiliating capitulation of the city to the Prussians, on 28 January 1871, by Adolphe Thiers and the newly formed Third Republic. The Commune numbered among its ranks radical intellectuals like Jules Vallès and the realist artist Gustave Courbet but the vast majority of its supporters were drawn from 'le petit peuple de Paris' who, in an act of defiance against the new regime (which had abandoned the city and established the National Assembly at Versailles), set up their own revolutionary government. Only ten weeks after its triumphant declaration at the Hôtel de Ville on 18 March 1871, however, the Commune was brutally crushed by the forces of the regular French army (the Versaillais), during what became known as *la semaine sanglante* (21 to 28 May 1871). In just seven days, the repression left some 20,000 people dead and parts of the city devastated by fire. Of the many 'lieux de mémoire' associated with the Commune, it was Père-Lachaise, the great cemetery in the east of the city, which proved the most enduring. The cemetery quickly became mythologized by the Commune's detractors as well as by some of its supporters as the setting for the last battle of the civil war but, as contemporary and modern historians have noted, the final engagements actually took place the next day, 28 May. And, on 29 May the Versaillais returned repeatedly to Père-Lachaise with groups of between 150 and 300 captured members of the Communard National Guard (*fédérés*) (most of whom had already surrendered), along with many civilians, including women and children. After lining their hostages up against the Mur de Charonne (today's *Mur des fédérés*), the troops executed them by machine-gun. The bodies fell into the long, deep ditch especially dug for the purpose in front of the wall, and those who were not killed outright were finished off in the ditch itself. Their task over, the soldiers hastily buried the corpses with the result that the exact number of people killed is not known.[4] The trials, executions, and deportation of anyone believed to have taken part in the Commune continued until 1875 and ex-Communards were not granted amnesty until 1880.

Despite the fact that *Le Monde illustré* was celebrated for its accurate and honest reporting,[5] in practice, the journal was no different from other newspapers, which, as Pierre Albert reminds us are 'agents de la propagation des idées et de la formation des opinions, [et] instruments de socialisation des individus.'[6] With the newspapers of the Third Republic specifically in mind, it is also interesting to note that Marcel Proust (at first sight perhaps an unusual commentator), goes further and claims that the press of this period was even more influential than the education system or the Church in what he considered to be the insidious promulgation of official ideology.[7] However, if official ideology can be promulgated via newspapers, so can unofficial, counter-ideologies. It is hardly surprising, therefore, that, throughout the Second Empire, the press, and illustrated newspapers in particular because of their perceived natural appeal to the illiterate, had been the subject of strict censorship. Article 22 of the Decree of 17 April 1852 specifically stated that anyone wishing to print or sell newspapers, books or illustrations and photographs of any kind was first required to register these with the

Ministry of the Interior or Prefect of Police. For the illustrated press this restriction effectively amounted to a form of direct censorship.[8] The role played by the left-wing radical press during the Commune appeared to confirm the perceived causal link between newspapers and insurrection and, within days of the end of the *semaine sanglante*, the new regime began rigorously to enforce the Decree of 1852 in an attempt to quell the overwhelming free circulation and trade in thousands of images relating to the events and personalities connected with the Commune. It was against this climate of strict censorship that the following articles and illustrations appeared in *Le Monde illustré* in the aftermath of May 1871.

The first article I would like to consider is Charles Monselet's piece for the regular feature, the *Courrier de Paris*, which was written after the Versaillais victory but which appeared in a posthumous edition of the journal dated 27 May 1871.[9] Monselet's account of the death throes of the Commune is a useful place to start because it draws on virtually all of the anti-revolutionary fears, obsessions, and clichés of his age and class.[10] For example: the Commune is a 'monument insigne de folies, de mensonges, de niaiseries et de férocités' to be compared with the 'trébuchements de la civilisation' of 1789; its supporters are 'ces législateurs fantoches, ces gouvernants sortis de la baraque de Guignol', mindlessly spouting the old clichés of 'quarte-vingt-treize'; and the destruction of Paris is to be compared with the sacking and burning of decadent imperial Rome by the barbarians or the perceived divine retribution meted out to London during the Great Fire ('ces incendies qui rappellent les incendies de Rome et de Londres').

Monselet relates how he witnessed 'la dévastation de ce centre [de Paris] [...] et répétant de minute en minute avec Shakespeare: «Horrible! Horrible!»', and how, finally, 'le drame monstrueux est allé s'achever dans un cimetière, comme le dernier acte d'*Hamlet*.' The reference to *Hamlet* enables Monselet to allude poetically to Père-Lachaise and, by association, to the massacre that took place there, whilst significantly omitting to report any of the grisly details. *Hamlet* is also particularly apposite since this tragedy deals with many of the same moral issues raised by the Commune: fratricide, honour, revenge, and political order.[11] Shakespeare's protagonist, since he is presented as a sympathetic character, is not perceived by the audience at the end of the play as having committed any sin. If he is to be blamed for anything, it is that he should have taken control of the situation and exacted revenge sooner, thereby avoiding so many unnecessary deaths. The parallel, oblique as it may at first appear, is with Thiers who, whilst the majority of the bourgeoisie supported him, was nevertheless criticized by some for his retreat from Paris and his failure to deal effectively with the insurrection early on.[12]

Monselet's overt literary references may be to Shakespeare, but his declamatory and poetic prose with its personification of death, extensive use of anaphora and alliteration, brings it closer to the rhetoric of Corneille:

> Ô mort! voilà bientôt dix mois que tu t'es abattue sur la France; voilà bientôt dix mois que ta large faux n'a cessé de se promener sur nos champs. Tantôt tu nous apparais, guerrière farouche, coiffée du casque de l'invasion; tantôt furie de faubourg, cachant dans un cabas fétide l'essence incendiaire; tantôt enfin, justicière implacable, fusillant contre un mur de pâles troupeaux de fédérés.

The melodramatic style of this passage recalls that of tragedies such as *Horace*, *Cinna* and *Polyeucte*, all of which were to be much performed as the decade progressed.[13] The moral and political issues debated in *Horace*, in particular, have much in common again with those of 1870-71, whilst Paris, like classical Rome, had also suffered at the hands of her internal and external enemies.[14]

By appealing to the shared political and cultural values of his implied readers, and through his use of what the sociologist and collective memory theorist Maurice Halbwachs would call, 'un langage fait des "mots de la tribu", d'un "lexique familial"', Monselet is able to rationalize and, by extension, excuse, Thiers' repression.[15]

Shakespearian allusions and Cornelian-style rhetoric are put to much the same use in the piece entitled 'La Dernière étape des fédérés au Père-Lachaise', which appeared under the pseudonym Léo de Bernard in the edition dated 24 June 1871 to accompany the front page illustration by Albert Robida entitled, 'L'Agonie de la Commune. – Marins, infanterie de marine et 74° de ligne purgeant le Père-Lachaise des derniers insurgés, le samedi 27 mai à 8 heures du soir' (figure 1).[16] The account is even structured like a five-act tragedy. The first few paragraphs provide the exposition of the 'drama', introduce the 'characters', and culminate in the customary note of suspense and expectation: 'Dans tout Paris on se demande avec angoisse quand finira ce second bombardement'. During the second 'act', the battle is played out through the night: 'la vigueur de l'attaque et l'acharnement de la riposte dénotent assez que le dénouement approche; que le drame va jouer son dernier acte sanglant.' The third 'act' is punctuated by the desertion of some of the Communards. Then, as befits a true classical tragedy, the fourth part of the text reports on the struggle and ultimate defeat of the *fédérés* by the Versaillais among the tombs of Père-Lachaise:

> La lutte suprême dans laquelle l'insurrection a exhalé, avec son dernier cri de haine, son dernier soupir, a été livrée au milieu des tombeaux de Charles Nodier, d'Emile Souvestre, de Balzac.
>   Le combat a eu lieu à arme blanche, et ce sont les troupes de marine qui ont donné les coups de la fin. Notre gravure reproduit cet épisode sanglant où la Commune a brûlé sa dernière amorce.

The reference to Nodier, Souvestre, and Balzac serves to highlight the difference between 'civilized' France and the 'groupe de forcenés' who are led, not by a Frenchman, but, significantly, by an unnamed 'colonel polonais'.[17] The slaughter, as is to be expected, takes place 'off-stage'. We only have the journalist's sanitized version of what happens: 'le vraisemblable' as opposed to 'le vrai'.

Albert Robida's illustration, like the text, shows little of the real horror of the so-called 'dernière étape' (just a few corpses in the foreground), and nothing at all of the subsequent massacres at Père-Lachaise (which had taken place before this edition of the journal went to press). The suppression of the full story could be seen as an attempt by *Le Monde illustré* to protect the delicate sensibilities of its readers or, more likely, as a form of self-censorship and as an early attempt at revisionism in line with official propaganda. However, taken purely on its own merits, Robida's illustration shows the *fédérés* in a positive light, unlike the majority of his sketches of the period which depict the Communards as drunken, lazy, and undisciplined soldiers.[18] Robida's *fédérés*, particularly the central figure, appear strong and heroic, quite unlike the 'forcenés' emitting their 'dernier cri de haine', as described in the textual account. Like most of the writers and artists of the period, Robida was unsympathetic to the Commune but no less appalled and sickened by the indiscriminate slaughter by the Versaillais of so many innocent people once the armed struggle was over.[19] This may have had a bearing on the way he chose to represent the Communards here.

'Act five' of the reported tragedy opens with a description of the dawn breaking after the final agony:

> Le jour se levait transparent. Le ciel était bleu; les arbustes et les plantes exhalaient leurs parfums du matin et leur feuillage printanier semblait plus verdoyant sous les rayons d'un soleil éclatant.
>
> La nature souriait au milieu des tombes et la faux de la mort, tout ensanglantée, se reposait un moment.

The corpses, still covered in their tattered uniforms are buried in the communal ditch and the reader is left in no doubt that the Communards, guilty of hubris, have brought about their own downfall: 'ces cadavres étaient ceux des fédérés pris les armes à la main et passés par les armes. On pouvait compter seize cent à peut près'. This figure may well be fairly accurate, but the implication that all those who died did so as a result of armed combat and the reporter's silence concerning the summary executions of 29 May seems to be a deliberate attempt to censor the facts.

The reader's pity is to be aroused, not by the spectacle of the dead *fédérés*, but by the description of the grief-stricken women and children they leave behind. Finally, there is catharsis and the delivery of the (reactionary) moral:

> Et les oiseaux se poursuivaient de branche en branche, gazouillant leurs petits cris joyeux.
>
> Ah ! que les horreurs de la guerre civile sont atroces devant ce calme inconscient de la nature, devant cette imperturbable sérénité de la création, qui ne semble si puissante que lorsqu'elle accuse l'inanité humaine.

As Paul Lidsky observes, it is difficult to produce a counter-revolutionary epic of the Commune when the 'heroes', Thiers and the Versaillais, are such unromantic and unsympathetic characters.[20] And yet, by its appropriation of the high genre of classical French tragedy, this account of the final triumph of the Versaillais over the doomed *fédérés* achieves just that. The article is effectively a 'minor epic' that manages to aestheticize and legitimize the brutality of the Versaillais reaction. Robert Tombs's judgement of *La Débâcle*, Emile Zola's full-blown counter-revolutionary novel of the Commune, is equally applicable to this journalistic account: 'the Commune ceases to be a political conflict and becomes an allegory. This permitted an optimistic conclusion round the themes of redemption and renewal.'[21]

The article's conclusion is fully consistent with the conservative bourgeois mood of the time which sought a rapid return to a sense of political, social and moral stability. And, if this meant supporting Thiers and thus apparently condoning his violent suppression of the Commune, then so be it. The belief that life must, and will go on, is further reinforced, intentionally or not, by the fact that this theatrical account of the defeat of the Commune is followed by something as banal as Monselet's *feuilleton, Chanvallon: histoire d'un passant sous le consulat et l'Empire*, which appears on the same page and contains a review of a Marivauesque comedy at the Comédie française entitled, *Venez, je m'ennuie!*.

A piece entitled 'Les Journées de mai: Paris en feu', which appears in *Le Monde illustré* on 7 October 1871 signed with the initials 'M.V.' (representing the pseudonym Maxime Vauvert), employs some of the same melodramatic, cliché-ridden rhetoric as the texts by Monselet and the journalist calling him/herself Léo de Bernard, but in this text there is a marked shift away from 'factual' reporting towards the evocation of the sheer, dramatic beauty of the city in flames:[22]

> Ce tableau de Paris en feu, dont nous tâchons de donner une idée aujourd'hui en choisissant l'un des sites [la Seine] où il fut le plus horriblement grand et pittoresque, dépasse tout ce que le rêve d'un peintre-poête pourrait imaginer.

Paris thus becomes the stage-setting for a Manichean battle between good and the evil. The fact that the city's churches and those buildings representative of French civilization, such as the Louvre and the Institut, have survived the 'foudres lancées par les génies de la destruction', whilst those associated with the 'decadent' Second Empire, such as the Tuileries, have been destroyed, is seen to be the result of divine intervention:

> Comment croire que la Sainte Chapelle, cette châsse sainte, cette relique artistique, resterait invulnérable au milieu même d'un foyer ardent? Et Saint-Germain-l'Auxerrois, et Saint-Gervais, ces précieux sanctuaires, et Notre-Dame, la vieille basilique [...] n'est ce pas par miracle que tout cela devait échapper?

The journalist's vision of the future is again optimistic. His or her version of apocalypse is more in keeping with the New, rather than the Old, Testament, with the Revelation rather than with the burning of Sodom and Gomorrah. Those 'génies de la destruction' (an allusion to Napoleon III and the Communards), have been overthrown and Paris, like Rome, through its acceptance of God and the Catholic Church, will be saved.

The piece concludes with a description of François Chifflart's accompanying illustration entitled, 'Histoire de Paris. – Les nuits de mai' (figure 2.):[23]

> M. Chifflart, dans la magnifique page que nous reproduisons aujourd'hui, a voulu reproduire ces idées. Qu'il nous soit permis de dire que nous qui les avons vus et ressentis, nous les retrouvons en jetant les yeux sur son tableau.
>
> Que si quelque autre témoin vient dire qu'il y manque la taille et la couleur, nous lui répondrons que, pour peindre ces choses, il faudrait pour toile l'étendue du ciel et pour couleur la palette de Satan.

Given its dramatic impact, it is surprising that few modern commentators have discussed Chifflart's 'Histoire de Paris. – Les nuits de mai' in any detail, and that the illustration is typically reproduced in miniature.[24] In its original setting, in the centre fold of the large-format *Le Monde illustré*, Chifflart's illustration is truly impressive; its power is heightened by the fact that it is followed by the usual lightweight items carried by the journal and by the intensity of the black and white reproduction, which serves to strengthen the symbolic charge of the dark flames and swirling clouds of smoke, rendering these even more fantastical. The Louvre, the twin towers of Notre-Dame, and the spires and domes of the churches are silhouetted against a clear, white horizon whilst the burning buildings representative of the Second Empire are seen to disappear beneath thick, dark clouds. Chifflart's drawing with its inclusion of two, barely discernible, 'génies de la destruction' in the heavens above the city (see detail in figure 3), recalls the juxtapositions of medieval imagery and modern Paris in, for example, Charles Meryon's *Le Vampire* (1853), Alphonse Chigot's *La Bourse* (1857), and Felicien Rops's vision of Satan sowing evil grain (depicted as naked women), over a city which the Church has ceased to control. Chifflart's imagery may be Romantic but his rendering of the reflection of light on the waters of the Seine owes much to Impressionism, whilst his swirling clouds look forward to Symbolist and Expressionist paintings such as Van Gogh's *The Starry Night* and Munch's *The Scream*.

According to Hélène Millot, representations of the Commune such as Chifflart's 'Histoire de Paris. – Les nuits de mai' constitute a denial of history.[25] Certainly, such illustrations with their biblical imagery would have appealed to a humiliated and angry nation seeking redemption for the 'sins' committed by the Empire and 'unpatriotic' revolutionaries. However, one could also argue that, rather than a denial of history, Chifflart's illustration merely exemplifies *l'Ordre moral*'s selective use of history. In *La Mémoire collective*, Halbwachs posits that official history is the creation of a society's dominant minority.[26] Thus, when a social group is in the process of creating and establishing its own system of values (be they religious, moral or aesthetic), it will try to diffuse these across all the other social groups which make up the nation as a whole. If these values succeed in becoming universally recognized and accepted, then, according to Halbwachs, they become an integral part of that nation's identity and consciousness. There is no doubt that images such as Chifflart's played an important part in such a process in the early years of the Republic. After all, it was not just the reactionaries who sought to deny the political and social grievances that gave rise to the Commune, but also many moderate Republicans too. What is even more interesting, however, is that Chifflart had actually fought alongside the Communards, and yet he appears to have envisaged the Commune in the same aesthetic, apocalyptic, and 'apolitical' terms as the conservatives and reactionaries. Perhaps the 'génies de la destruction' should be re-cast as the Furies and made to represent the Versaillais.

On the 28 December 1871, in his capacity as Military Governor General of Paris, General Ladmirault (one of the commanders responsible for the repression of the city during the *semaine sanglante*), signed a new Decree banning the sale or exhibition on the streets of Paris of all drawings, photographs, or emblems deemed by the censors to be 'de nature à troubler l'ordre public'.[27] Aesthetic representations of Paris in flames or in ruins, and photomontages of Communard prisoners awaiting trial or of Communards killing priests, however, seemed able to evade censorship, at least until 1872-3.[28] But by then, the right-wing myth of Paris and the Commune that *Le Monde illustré* had done so much to promulgate, was firmly fixed in the collective psyche.

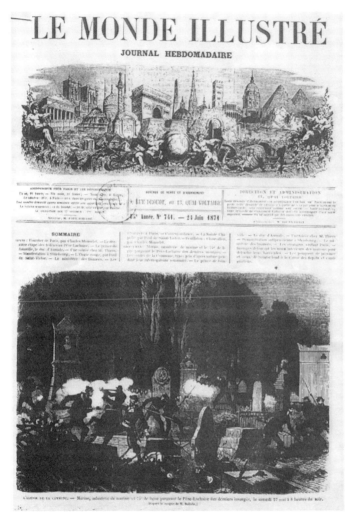

Figure 1
'L'AGONIE DE LA COMMUNE.-
Marins, infanterie de marine et 74 de ligne purgeant le Père-Lachaise des
derniers insurgés, le samedi 27 mai à 8 heures du soir. (D'après le croquis
de M. Robida)'.

Figure 2.
'HISTOIRE DE PARIS.- LES NUITS DE MAI.- (Dessin de M.
Chifflart)'.

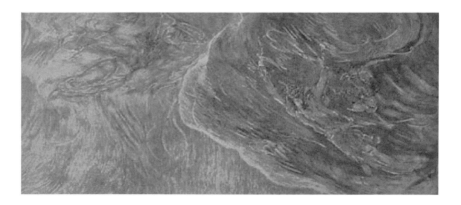

Figure 3
Detail of Chifflart's 'Histoire de Paris. Les Nuits de mai.

NOTES

[1] This study develops in a different (but related) perspective, the subject of my PhD thesis, *Urban Topography and the Collective Memory: Paris and the Commune 1871 to 1878* (Royal Holloway, University of London), to be submitted in the autumn of 2003. See also my, '*Une Page d'amour*: un panorama politique', *Les Cahiers naturalistes*, 76 (2002), 177-91.

[2] The majority of works on the press of the Third Republic are general histories. See, for example, Claude Bellanger and others, *Histoire générale de la presse française*, vols ii and iii (Presses Universitaires de France, 1972), and Irene Collins, *The Government and the Newspaper Press in France, 1814-1881* (Oxford University Press, 1959). Whilst the illustrations reproduced in *Le Monde illustré* form part of a general corpus of Franco-Prussian War and Commune imagery, commentators have invariably divorced these from their accompanying texts, thus overlooking the potential for further interpretative analysis. See, for example, Albert Boime, *Art and the French Commune: Imagining Paris after War and Revolution* (Princeton University Press, 1995).

[3] For a detailed history of the Commune see Robert Tombs, *The Paris Commune, 1871* (Longman, 2000), and William Serman, *La Commune de Paris (1871)* (Fayard, 1986).

[4] Communard accounts of the massacre put the total number of those executed at about 1,900 people. See Serman, pp. 510-11 and 523, and Tombs, pp. 11-12 and 195. On the myth of the *Mur*, see Madeleine Rebérioux, 'Le Mur des fédérés: Rouge, "sang craché"', in *Les Lieux de mémoire, I, La République*, ed. Pierre Nora (Gallimard, 1986), pp. 619-49.

[5] Eugène Dubief, *Le Journalisme* (Hachette, 1892), p. 235.

[6] *La Presse française* (La Documentation française, 1990), p. 30.

[7] Michael Sprinker, *History and Ideology in Proust: 'A la recherche du temps perdu' and the Third French Republic* (Cambridge University Press, 1994), pp. 45-47.

[8] Collins, pp. 122 and 164-68; and Donald E. English, *Political Uses of Photography in the Third French Republic, 1871-1914* (Ann Arbor, 1981), p. 65.

[9] Charles Monselet (1825-1888), is perhaps most famous for his works on gastronomy but his prodigious output covers a range of genres including novels, poetry, history, and journalism. He contributed several articles and *feuilletons* to *le Monde illustré* in 1870-71.

[10] See Paul Lidsky, *Les écrivains contre la Commune* (La Découverte, 1999); J. M. Roberts, 'La Commune considérée par la droite: dimensions d'une mythologie', *Revue d'histoire moderne et contemporaine*, XIX (1972), 187-205; A.E. Carter, *The Idea of Decadence in French Literature: 1830-1900* (University of Toronto Press, 1958); and Koenraad W. Swart, *The Sense of Decadence in Nineteenth-Century France* (Martinus Nijhoff, 1964).

[11] For further examples of the Commune as Shakespearian tragedy, see Catulle Mendès, *Les 73 journées de la Commune (du 18 mars au 20 mai 1871)* (E. Lachaud éd., 1871), p. 292, and Victor Fournel, *Paris et ses ruines en mai 1871* (Charpentier, 1872), pp. i-vi.

[12] See, for example, Maxime Du Camp, *Les Convulsions de Paris*, 4 vols, 5th edn (Hachette, 1881), II, 11.

[13] See M. Descotes, *Les Grands rôles du théâtre de Corneille* (Presses Universitaires de France, 1962). Corneille featured high on the list of authors studied throughout the nineteenth century. See also A. Delapierre and A. P. Delamarche's *Exercices de mémoire* (1887) which, as Matt Matsuda suggests, exhibits 'a canon of renowned French writers [including Corneille] [...], a proud carefully managed self-portrait of a literary tradition emphasizing national loyalty, prudence, and the spirit of finesse.' *The Memory of the Modern*, (Oxford University Press, 1996), pp. 68-69.

[14] See, for example, Camille's speech in Act IV, scene 6, ll.1309-19.

[15] *Les Cadres sociaux de la mémoire*, ed. Gérard Namer (Albin Michel, 1997), p. 349.

[16] 'Léo de Bernard' is a non-attributed pseudonym shared among the journalists of *Le Monde illustré*. See *Dictionnaire des pseudonymes*, ed. Georges d'Heylli (Slatkine reprints, 1971), p. 43. Albert Robida (1848-1926) covered the Prussian Siege of Paris and the Commune for *Le Monde illustré* before subsequently moving to *La Vie Parisienne*, and, in 1880, founding his own paper, *La Caricature*. See Philippe Brun, *Albert Robida (1848-1926): sa vie, son œuvre suivi d'une bibliographie complète de ses écrits et dessins* (Promodis, 1984), and Fred Robida, 'Albert Robida en 1870-71', *Documents sur la Commune, Europe*, XIX (1971), 63-75.

[17] This could be a reference to Jaroslaw Dombrowski (1836-71), one of the Commune's chief military commanders. However, Dombrowski had already been wounded on 23 May at the barricade on the rue Myrrha and subsequently died at the Larivoisière hospital. It is not known where his body was buried. See Bernard Noël, *Dictionnaire de la Commune*, 2 vols (Flammarion, 1978), I, 213-14.

[18] See his *Album du Siège et de la Commune*, ed. Lucien Scheler, 2 vols (Librairie Historique & Librairie Thomas-Scheler, 1971), II.

[19] *Album du Siège*, I, 62.

[20] Lidsky, *Les écrivains contre la Commune*, pp. 93-94.

[21] Tombs, *The Paris Commune*, p. 194.

[22] *Dictionnaire des pseudonymes*, p. 43.

[23] Nicholas-François Chifflart (1825-1901), winner of the prestigious Prix de Rome in 1851, contributed a number of illustrations to *Le Monde illustré*. These were subsequently published in album form by the journal. See Valérie Sueur, *François Chifflart graveur et illustrateur* (Réunion des Musées nationaux, 1994), and Louis Noël, *François Chifflart: peintre et graveur français, 1825-1901* (Imprimerie Vandroth-Fauconnier, 1902).

[24] For example, Hélène Millot, 'Une Commune fin de siècle? *Les Oiseaux s'envolent et les fleurs tombent* d'Élémir Bourges', in *Écrire la Commune: Témoignages, récits et romans (1871-1931)*, ed. Roger Bellet and Philippe Régnier (Éditions du Lérot, 1994), p. 194, and John Milner, *Art, War and Revolution in France 1870-1871: Myth, Reportage and Reality* (Yale University Press, 2000), pp. 172-3.

[25] Millot, 'Une Commune fin de siècle?', p. 195.

[26] ed. Gérard Namer (Albin Michel, 1997), ch. 4.

[27] Archives nationales, reference F18 2363. See also English, *Political Uses of Photography*, pp. 67-69.

[28] English, pp. 67-69.

PART III:
MARGINALIZATION AND TRANSGRESSION IN MODERN FRENCH LITERATURE

Gide's (non-)Bite at the Forbidden Fruit

Victoria Reid
University of Reading

Gide's forays into the forbidden are well known: for example, he is the earliest writer in France to write in the first person about his homosexuality; on his 1936 return from the USSR he breaks ranks by speaking out against the regime. Our focus, however, will not be on such ruptures with convention, but rather on two self-imposed and co-dependent forbidden fruit in Gide, namely the notion that his pederasty might harm, and second, that of the sexual woman.

Roger Martin du Gard records his meeting with Gide of 31 July 1931:

> Je trouve Gide bouleversé. Il me montre une brochure où il est accusé de 'pervertir la jeunesse'. Rien ne l'émeut, ne l'indigne, ne le désespère davantage. [...] '"Pervertir la jeunesse", cela veut dire, en clair : *faire de jeunes invertis*, profiter de leur complaisance, de leur passivité.... [...] Que de fois j'ai été retenu par le respect que m'inspire un être jeune ! J'ai souvent attendu des mois avant d'accepter une tendresse qui s'offrait... [...] Croyez-moi, cher ! Je puis me rendre cette justice : [...] mon rôle a toujours été moralisateur [...] Combien de garçons, engagés sur de mauvaises pentes, ai-je ramenés dans le droit chemin, qui, sans moi, se seraient abandonnés à leurs instincts les plus vils, et se seraient définitivement dévoyés ! [...]' Rien, selon lui, [...] autant que les révélations d'un camarade plus âgé ne peut aider l'enfant à franchir, sans dommage, dans une atmosphère de mâle et de fraternelle ferveur, le seuil redoutable de la puberté. Seule, une telle initiation est capable de le détourner des pernicieuses tentations du trottoir, de lui épargner l'avilissante – et dangereuse – découverte du plaisir 'sur le lit d'une prostituée'...[1]

Gide defends his sexuality vigorously, suggesting perhaps that 'the lady doth protest too much'. Certainly his faith in the altruism and ennobling power of his pederasty must be questioned if we consider the calculation he employs in avoiding any suggestion that his sexuality might be nefarious or profit from a power position based on age, race, wealth or class. Steel details, for example, how *Corydon*, Gide's pseudo-scientific treatise on homosexuality, omits to mention the accusation made against Socrates that he corrupted the young, although elsewhere the relation of the philosopher's pederasty to his intellectual creativity *is* developed, and, also, how, 'Il faut que le scandale arrive', the provocative rallying cry from *Le Traité du Narcisse*, fails to engage more fully with the biblical context that inspired it,[2] that is, the judgement in *Matthew* that 'whoever causes one of these little ones who believe in me to sin, it would be better for him to have a great millstone fastened round his neck and to be drowned in the depth of the sea'.[3] We might follow Goulet's lead when he exposes *la mauvaise foi* of the pastor of *La Symphonie pastorale* by substituting 'le Pasteur' for Edouard's name in the following passage from *Les Faux-Monnayeurs*, by using Gide's name instead:[4]

> Ce qui ne me plaît pas chez [*Gide*], ce sont les raisons qu'il se donne. Pourquoi cherche-t-il à se persuader […] qu'il conspire au bien de[*s enfants*] ? Mentir aux autres, passe encore ; mais à soi-même ! Le torrent qui noie un enfant prétend-il lui porter à boire ? Je ne nie pas qu'il y ait, de par le monde, des actions nobles, généreuses, et même désintéressées ; je dis seulement que derrière le plus beau motif, souvent se cache un diable habile et qui sait tirer gain de ce qu'on croyait lui ravir. ([*Romans*], 1109.)

The Gospel's punishment of drowning the perpetrator is a fitting riposte to the crime of drowning a child. Yet in Gide's texts, as in his quoted defence, the victim status of younger sexual partners is elided: the older man is solicited by the boys and money transactions go unrepresented.[5] By claiming to rescue boys from the clutches of diseased women the pederast plays the moralist.

The Bite

Gide's autobiography, *Si le grain ne meurt...*(1920), relates the earliest manifestation of the young André's disgust at female flesh:[6]

> 'Va vite embrasser ta cousine', me dit ma mère […]. (Je ne devais avoir guère plus de quatre ans ; cinq peut-être.) Je

m'avançai. La cousine de Flaux m'attira contre elle en se baissant, ce qui découvrit son épaule. Devant l'éclat de cette chair, je ne sais quel vertige me prit : au lieu de poser mes lèvres sur la joue qu'elle me tendait, fasciné par l'épaule éblouissante j'y allai d'un grand coup de dent. La cousine fit un cri de douleur, j'en fis un d'horreur ; puis je crachai, plein de dégoût. On m'emmena bien vite, et je crois qu'on était si stupéfait qu'on oublia de me punir.[7]

A similar incident is related in Freud's 'The Rat Man', which Gide may have read.[8] Freud asks the Rat Man to recall a childhood sexual misdemeanour for which his father had punished him. The psychoanalyst thinks that this will explain why his patient unconsciously casts his father in the role of 'an interferer with [his] sexual enjoyment'. The Rat Man recalls being beaten for a misdemeanour and retaliating angrily by hurling abuse at his father: 'The patient subsequently questioned his mother again. She confirmed the story, adding that at the time he had been between three and four years old and that he had been given the punishment because he had *bitten* someone', possibly his nurse.[9] The Rat Man's punishment stops him from masturbating and Freud views this 'catastrophic end' to infantile sexual activity as the catalyst for his obsessional neurosis. André, by contrast, is not punished at all, and his masturbation continues.[10]

Nevertheless, the 'bite' leads to a common resolution, inhibiting the heterosexual drive in both men. André and the Rat Man share a disgust of prostitutes and a concomitant dread of contracting syphilis.[11] The venom Gide shows towards prostitutes has been attributed to his 'terreur panique des maladies "vénériennes"!'.[12] The Rat Man sees rats as a symbol for both syphilitic infection and children, but the lady he loves is removed from this by being biologically condemned to childlessness (*Rat Man*, 94 & 97). Through association, therefore, she will be unable to infect him. Similarly, in Gide, the fictional incarnations of his wife, Madeleine, will be childless and apparently asexual.[13] Loved women are accordingly removed from sexual 'nastiness'.

The 'Nastiness' of Woman

Lucile Bucolin of *La Porte étroite*, the fictional incarnation of Madeleine Gide's mother, Mathilde Rondeau, embodies the carnal, sexually-aggressive and frightening female. She invites her nephew Jérôme to approach her and slides her hand inside his shirt. Her sexual dissipation is further reinforced when Jérôme spies her entertaining a lieutenant in his uncle's home, while her younger children play at the foot of the chaise longue (*La Porte*, 497-500; 503-04). This scene is inspired by real-life events, as a similar incident in Gide's autobiography reveals (*Slg*, 159 – 61). The fictional and autobiographical infidelity scenes reveal the harm such untrustworthy and sexually incontinent behaviour inflicts on an innocent: of Alissa Jérôme writes, 'je sentais intensément que cette détresse était beaucoup trop forte pour cette petite âme palpitante, pour ce frêle corps tout secoué de sanglots.'

The angelic female child is not the only victim: vulnerable boys, as Gide has warned us, also fall prey to these women. The build-up to both the Jérôme – Lucile shirt incident (*La Porte*) and the prostitute scenes in the autobiography expose the narrator's terror: lascivious Lucile wears low-cut 'corsages légers et largement ouverts'; her foster mother fears the girl's influence on her own children; Jérôme conjectures that her foster father, 'sans ressources contre l'intrigue et complètement désarmé devant le mal', would have struggled to bring up this Créole 'enfant si séduisante' in Le Havre (*La Porte*, 207-09). (Note the link between Lucile's first residence in France and 'le passage du Havre', the haunt of the Parisian prostitutes in *Si le grain*.[14]) Around his aunt Jérôme feels 'un singulier malaise', and his older-narrator-self judges Lucile to be guilty of having done 'tant de mal'.

In the autobiography a sense of apprehension surrounds *le passage du Havre*: André's mother warns him that *le passage* is 'extrêmement mal fréquenté'; André is 'tout troublé par ces énigmatiques paroles', and in his mind's eye sees the passage 'comme un lieux de stupre, une géhenne, le Roncevaux des bonnes mœurs'; the horror of the place obsesses him, and he imagines his friend Tissaudier 'orgiastiquement lacéré par les hétaïres'. When he asks Tissaudier if he has ever been to the passage, his friend's delayed response provokes a hysterical reaction in André: 'tout secoué de sanglots, me précipitant aux genoux de mon camarade: "Bernard! Oh ! Je t'en supplie : n'y va pas."' Yet Bernard's knowledge of 'le métier' incites André to 'prêter attention à certains spectacles de la rue'. When the adolescent sees the mysterious prostitutes on the street ahead of him, he braces himself and continues on his way. Fear gains the upper hand, however, when a prostitute bars his route. André about-turns and in a voice 'à la fois grondeuse, moqueuse, câline et enjouée', she calls out after him, 'Mais il ne faut pas avoir peur comme ça, mon joli garçon!', echoing Lucile's question, 'Pourquoi t'en vas-tu si vite? Jérôme ! est-ce que je te fais peur?'. Years later, André writes, 'ces quêtantes créatures m'inspiraient encore autant de terreur que des vitrioleuses'. Likewise Jérôme's anger towards Lucile still resonates (*La Porte*, 499).

Polarization

André is polarized from 'ces quêtantes créatures' and occupies the same space as the angelic Emmanuèle,[15] who, in turn, is polarized from her mother. Further, the real name of Gide's first cousin and future wife, Madeleine, avoids any impure associations with Mary Magdalen by being replaced in the autobiography with the angelic Emmanuèle, meaning 'God with us'. Similarly, Alissa, Jérôme's one-time soul mate, will be polarized from her mother, her sexuality minimized by emphasis on her spirituality (*La Porte*, 584). By aligning his fictional embodiments to an angelic figure, Gide promotes his own purity and strengthens his moral case.

In *Si le grain...* André and Emmanuèle's relationship proceeds through a fusion of tastes, thoughts and actions: she determines what food they will not eat; he, what books they will read. Emmanuèle is apparently removed from the tarnish of female sexuality because she has no dealings with 'les nourritures terrestres': in the episode at the dinner table, it is her *refusal* of food that is significant (*Slg*, 159). Similarly, in the *récit* Alissa's spirituality is emphasized from the outset, her arched eyebrows resembling those Jérôme imagines Dante's Beatrix to have had (*La Porte*, 501). Following the sermon about 'la porte étroite', Jérôme fantasizes that his disembodied unselfish self enters the doorway leading into Alissa's room, where he would experience 'une autre joie, pure, mystique, séraphique [...] comme une flamme aiguë où le cœur d'Alissa et le mien s'épuisaient' (505 – 06).

Poles Undermined

Yet this ethereal vision of Alissa relies on Jérôme being blinkered. Alissa's affinity to her mother is greater than Jérôme could accept: one evening Alissa is stretched out on the couch. Her father enters and is disorientated, momentarily believing her to be her mother. That same evening,

> Jérôme lisait par-dessus mon épaule, debout, appuyé contre mon fauteuil, penché sur moi. Je ne pouvais le voir mais sentais son haleine et comme la chaleur et le frémissement de son corps. Je feignais de continuer ma lecture, mais je ne comprenais plus ; je ne distinguais plus les lignes ; un trouble si étrange s'était emparé de moi que j'ai dû me lever de ma chaise, en hâte, tandis que je le pouvais encore. J'ai pu quitter quelques instants la pièce sans qu'heureusement il se soit rendu compte de rien... (*ibid.*, 585 – 86).

So much for the seraphic girl.[16]

Moreover, Jérôme's designation of Lucile as the evil object of his anger does not wholly disguise the fascination she holds for him. A process of curiosity, fascination and disgust can be traced, which compromises the subject who would rather cling to the disgust factor alone. The 'bite' scene and André's encounter with the prostitutes demonstrate curiosity (for his cousin's skin; for 'certains spectacles de la rue'), fascination ('l'éclat de cette chair'; 'allure bizarre de certaines femmes') and disgust (he spits, 'plein de dégoût'; 'ces quêtantes créatures' fill him with terror), and this also grafts onto Jérôme's dealings with Lucile: he is eager to discover what she is reading; he questions his mother about her origins and makes his own conjectures. That he conserves her portrait, picks up her book and offers her his hand ('Le cœur battant, je m'approche d'elle; je prends sur moi de lui sourire et de lui tendre la main' [*La Porte*, 500]), indicates that he is as fascinated as he is frightened by her, confirming the mixed feeling 'd'admiration et d'effroi' she elicits in him. A fetishistic attraction apparently infuses his fascination: like Freud's patient who endows noses 'at will with the luminous shine which was not perceptible to others', Jérôme explains how '[Lucile] portait parfois à son front, pourtant parfaitement mat, un mouchoir comme pour essuyer une moiteur.'[17] Additionally, he may have been sniffing her handkerchief, 'dont m'émerveillaient la finesse et l'odeur'.[18] When he picks up a book she has dropped, 'en voyant que c'étaient des vers, je rougis'. His unexplained embarrassment could result from a sense of being compromised: later Jérôme will reveal his own love of poetry by reading Baudelaire aloud to Alissa, and presumably a common passion amongst nephew, mother and daughter would unsettle a boy who later strives to reduce 'en pure haine le sentiment complexe et indécis encore que j'éprouvais pour Lucile Bucolin' (*La Porte*, 517). After Lucile touches him Jérôme tries to purge himself of her: 'je trempai mon mouchoir, l'appliquai sur mon front, lavai, frottai mes joues, mon cou, tout ce que cette femme avait touché'. Unfortunately he fails to expel her from him entirely, his wetter, faster actions frenziedly echoing her languorous dabbing.

Gide: the 'nasty' woman

Such undermining culminates in Madeleine's comparison of the adult Gide to Mathilde Rondeau. In 1918 Madeleine is forced to explicitly acknowledge Gide's homosexuality. Devastated by Gide's public display of his love affair with Marc Allégret, Madeleine burns the letters Gide sent her during their youth. Two years later, Gide recalls an instance which might have indicated his homosexuality to Madeleine prior to 1918. Gide, addressing his friend Schlumberger, first details how the isolation of Cuverville, his Normandy home affects him: 'certains jours, le désir me fait errer comme un insensé à travers la maison, et sortir, et courir dans les champs comme un possédé, vers les petits bergers, vers les enfants qui jouent dans les ruisseaux.'[19] He adds, 'Il faut aussi vous dire que, autrefois, lorsque ma femme était encore une toute jeune fille, un scandale domestique avait détruit le ménage de ses parents [...] et cette découverte lui avait causée alors un tel ébranlement, ce secret avait été si lourd à porter pendant sa jeunesse, que sa sensibilité, malgré le temps passé, en conservait encore l'empreinte.' (Schlumberger must have been reminded of the episodes related in *La Porte étroite* and *Si le grain....*). Then comes the crux: 'Donc, une année que je m'étais pris d'intérêt pour un fils du jardinier, que j'attirais le bambin dans la maison, que je cherchais à le faire travailler, ma femme m'a dit, un soir, en me regardant avec une expression de supplication anxieuse : "Il ne faut pas que, dans notre maison, « nous ayons encore à rougir... »"'.[20] Such a confession, if it is that, sits strangely with Gide's self-defence of his pederasty, outlined in the introduction. Instead of an impassioned self-defence, Gide here leaves the accusation unanswered, offering only the feeble defence that he means no harm to the children, merely wanting to see them, 'de les faire causer, de les imaginer nus, de les avoir autour de moi', contrasting with the concrete harm caused by Mathilde Rondeau's infidelity. Gide's contextualization of the accusation presents his wife's response as an overreaction. Yet in his writing he too dwells on the wickedness of Mathilde's textual avatars, not only representing the pain inflicted on Alissa / Emmanuèle, but also using the wicked women to obliquely support the idea that pederasty is beneficent, protecting young boys, who otherwise might be scarred, like Jérôme by Lucile.

Gide is again identified with the sexually aggressive woman by François Reymond, a fifteen-year-old who rebuffs the sexual advances of the seventy-two-year-old author.[21] In *L'Envers du Journal de Gide*, Reymond recounts Gide's attempted seduction of him, comparing it to Lucile's attempted seduction of Jérôme.[22] Most strikingly, just as Jérôme runs off to the tap to scrub every part of him Lucile had touched, François immediately runs to the bathroom to wash away Gide's touch.

Refuge: the non-bite

But how can Gide decontaminate himself from himself? One strategy is to fuel the notion of an eternally pure realm, which has the power to reinstate innocence. Gide maintains that a homosexual's love for woman cannot be surpassed, as it is 'dégagé de toutes les contingences sexuelles' and has 'quelque chose d'embaumé contre quoi le temps n'a plus de prise...'[23] This fantasy of a non-contingent world is further conveyed through the topos of Eden before the Fall: in André and Emmanuèle's dawn walks around the grounds of La Roque the couple, hand in hand, experience 'un éden quotidien avant l'éveil de l'homme et la somnolence du jour' (*Slg*, 219); in *Le Voyage d'Urien*, Urien longs to be united with the good Ellis who waits for him 'au delà des temps, où les neiges sont éternelles' (*Romans*, 60); and in *Le Traité du Narcisse* the '[c]haste Eden' is where all is still and beautifully configured. These paradises are precarious, however, and the third is lost when Adam breaks a branch from the tree of knowledge, causing the birth of time and of woman (*ibid.*, 6).

Sartre's Jonas Complex articulates this fantasy of eternal, renewable purity.[24] In *Narcisse,* abuse of the tree of knowledge destroys paradise and Sartre observes how the intake of knowledge is often expressed through 'métaphores alimentaires (absorption, digestion, assimilation)', implying a breaking-down process: once the knowledge is consumed it cannot be consumed again, just as virginity cannot be regained. Paradise is destroyed by the bite of the apple, or the breaking of a branch of the knowledge tree. Yet a work of art, as Sartre reveals, escapes this conundrum by remaining 'à la même place, indéfinement absorbé, mangé et indéfinement intact, tout entier digéré et cependant tout entier dehors, indigeste comme un caillou.' He continues, 'On remarquera l'importance dans les imaginations naïves du symbole du "digéré indigeste", le caillou dans l'estomac de l'autruche, Jonas dans l'estomac de la baleine. Il marque un rêve d'assimilation non destructrice.' In Gide's imaginary such a conception permits his intake of knowledge without digesting the apple or damaging the tree. He therefore can simultaneously bite the forbidden fruit, gain its knowledge/pleasure, and conserve his innocence by insisting that it remain intact.

This desire operates in sexual fantasy, as Sartre explains:

> Cette synthèse impossible de l'assimilation et de l'intégrité conservée de l'assimilé se rejoint, dans ses racines les plus profondes, avec les tendances fondamentales de la sexualité. La 'possession' charnelle en effet nous offre l'image irritante et séduisante d'un corps perpétuellement possédé et perpétuellement neuf, sur lequel la possession ne laisse aucune trace. C'est ce que symbolise profondément la qualité de 'lisse', de 'poli'. Ce qui est lisse peut se prendre, se tâter, et n'en demeure pas moins impénétrable, n'en fuit pas moins sous la caresse appropriative, comme l'eau. C'est pour quoi l'on insiste tant, dans les descriptions érotiques, sur la blancheur lisse du corps de la femme. Lisse : qui se reforme sous la caresse, comme l'eau se reforme sur le passage de la pierre qui l'a trouée.[25]

If Gide is to cling to the fantasy of a 'corps [...] perpétuellement neuf', he must first stress the non-possessive nature of his sexuality. This he does in his defence against accusations of perverting the youth: '"Pervertir la jeunesse!"... On sait bien, d'ailleurs, ce que les gens "normaux" entendent par là! Ce qu'ils supposent toujours !... Eux, quand ils courent après une femme, c'est pour la posséder'. Second, Gide must promote the women, fictional and real, who function as reserves of purity: communion with Alissa bathes Jérôme in her spiritual halo; love for Emmanuèle allows André to believe in his pure essence. It is perhaps telling that both Alissa of *La Porte étroite* and Ellis of *Le Voyage d'Urien* contain 'lisse' in their names. Their 'lisse' quality does not however eroticize them, but is rather appropriated by the male protagonist, who cloaks himself in the woman's smoothness to facilitate his fantasy of an eternally new, pure self. This tactic is evident in Gide's belief that Madeleine's action of burning *her* letters from him has robbed *him* of the purest part of his being: 'Ces lettres étaient le trésor de ma vie, le meilleur de moi [...] [l]e plus pur de mon existence, le plus pur de mon cœur' (*MAG*, 191–3). Gide has been stripped of his main source of detoxification.

Perhaps retaliation motivates Gide's subversion of André and Emmanuèle's Eden of La Roque. In Part 2 of the autobiography, written after the *crise* of 1918, a second Eden is lived by André, this time in El Kantara, North Africa. The location is already loaded: in Gide's *récit*, *L'Immoraliste* (1902), El Kantara is the unhallowed burial site of Marceline, Michel's Catholic wife.[26] Yet in *Si le grain...* André and his Arab servant and friend, Athman, spend 'dans cet éden deux jours paradisiaques, dont le souvenir n'a rien que de souriant et de pur' (*Slg*, 319). Intertextually, then, the male couple are walking over the woman's grave. Like La Roque's Eden, this one has no sexual element. However, the preceding paragraph in *Si le grain...* relates André's sexual liaison with Athman's brother, with whom André communicated principally through 'cette tendre façon qu[e Sadek] avait de me prendre les mains, de garder mes mains dans les siennes, ma main droite dans sa main droite, de sorte que nous continuions de marcher, les bras mutuellement croisés, silencieux comme des ombres'. Like the couples' intertwined arms, the sections of text separately concerning Athman and Sadek become interwoven: the affair with Sadek echoes, if not parodies, André and Emmanuèle's hand-holding and walking in the Eden of La Roque, while the platonic relation with Athman 'dans cet éden' purges the scene of sexual impurity by displacing the intimacy and pleasure with Sadek onto the non-sexual relationship with Athman. This purified Eden also purifies: André arrives on his first trip to Algeria a virgin; on his second he departs, despite considerable homosexual activity, with a memory that 'n'a rien que de souriant et de pur'.

When the child André bites his cousin's shoulder, he spits, 'plein de dégoût'. Metaphorically he has dared bite the apple, but his response has been quick enough to avert consuming the poison. Since Gide believes that 'possession' has no role in his practice of homosexuality, one could parallel the refusal to eat the apple / shoulder to the refusal to sexually possess another, refusals which nevertheless curiously permit gains of knowledge and pleasure. Gide protects the fantasy of a prelapsarian state by occupying a fortress comprising his perceived salutary and moral pederasty; his belief that his love of a good woman surpasses any heterosexual's love of her; and his nurturing of spiritual women in his writings. The citadel is under attack, however, from those who accuse Gide of perverting the innocent; sexual women who not only prey on his fictional selves, but occasionally force him to glimpse his predator-self; female characters who seep out of their pure spiritual mould; and a wife who burns his pure foundations. Unlike Eve Gide can bite the apple and still believe in his own purity: Gide's forbidden, it seems, is that which threatens his fantasy of the non-bite.

NOTES

[1] Roger Martin du Gard, *Notes sur André Gide* (Gallimard, 1951), pp. 95-98. Henceforth *RMG Notes*.
[2] David Steel, 'L'Enfance saisie dans *Si le grain ne meurt, Corydon* et *Les Faux-Monnayeurs*', *André Gide* 8 (1987), pp. 179-97 (p. 184-86).
[3] Matthew 18. 5-7.
[4] Alain Goulet, 'Ecrire *La Symphonie pastorale*', in *Lectures d'André Gide*, eds J-Y Debreuille & P Masson (Presses Universitaires de Lyon, 1994), p. 125.
[5] Naomi Segal, *André Gide: Pederasty and Pedagogy* (Clarendon, 1998), pp. 217-19.
[6] The name 'André' is used to distinguish the protagonist of the autobiography from Gide the author.
[7] *Si le grain ne meurt...* in André Gide, *Souvenirs et Voyages* (Gallimard, 2001), p. 82. Henceforward *Slg*.
[8] See Steel, 'L'Enfance', pp. 191-97. Gide inserts *Si le grain...* into the autobiographical canon by paralleling a similar 'biting' incident in Stendhal's *La vie d'Henri Brûlard*. In addition, the *Rat Man* analogy allows Gide to slot his work, essentially a 'coming out' text, into a 'scientific' scheme of sexual development.
[9] 'Notes upon a Case of Obsessional Neurosis (The "Rat Man")' (1909) in Sigmund Freud, *Case histories II* (Penguin, 1991), pp. 85-88. Henceforward *Rat Man*.
[10] André's masturbation at school and as a young adult is referred to on p. 121 and p. 309 of *Slg*.
[11] *Rat Man*, 39 & 94; *Slg*, 207-10 & 321.
[12] *RMG Notes*, 98. See also *Romans* (Gallimard, 1958),p. 40.
[13] Madeleine and André Gide themselves had a *mariage blanc*.
[14] This link is reinforced when André's mother first tells him of *le passage du Havre*: 'La voix de maman était grave, et elle fronçait les sourcils comme je me souviens que faisait

le capitaine du navire, certain jour de traversée orageuse entre Le Havre et Honfleur' (*Slg*, 206).

[15] Her mother's infidelity joins the couple together: André resolves to employ 'tout mon amour, toute ma vie' in alleviating Emmanuèle's distress (*Slg*, 160-61); Jérôme relates how his discovery of Alissa's grief 'décida de ma vie ; [...] je pressais [...] sur son front mes lèvres par où mon âme s'écoulait.' (*La Porte étroite* in *Romans*, 503-04).

[16] Peter Fawcett, for example, observes that Alissa is 'bien la fille de sa mère' (' "Le portrait de cette âme de femme" : Alissa dans *La Porte étroite*' in *Lectures d'André Gide*, p. 104).

[17] S. Freud, 'Fetishism'(1927) in *On Sexuality* (London: Penguin, 1991), p. 351.

[18] Elements in Jérôme's description intensify her fetishistic shimmer: 'parfois elle tirait de sa ceinture un minuscule *miroir à glissant couvercle d'argent*, qui pendait à *sa chaîne* de montre avec divers objets ; elle se regardait, d'un doigt touchait sa lèvre, cueillait *un peu de salive* et s'en *mouillait* le coin des *yeux*' [*my italics*] (*La Porte*, 499).

[19] Such behaviour offers a perverse contrast to Christ's words, 'Laissez venir à moi les petits enfants'.

[20] Jean Schlumberger, *Madeleine et André Gide* (Gallimard, 1956), p. 188. Henceforth *MAG*.

[21] Segal, 331-41.

[22] *ibid.*, 340.

[23] *MAG*, 193. See also *RMG Notes*, 112.

[24] Jean-Paul Sartre, *L'Être et le néant: Essai d'Ontologie phénoménologique*, (Gallimard, 1943), p. 667-9.

[25] This formulation echoes the jubilant defiance of Christ's words in *Le Traité du Narcisse* that, ' "Tout est consommé... "': '... Et puis, non! tout est à refaire, à refaire éternellement'.

[26] David Steel, 'A Death in the Desert: Gide's *L'Immoraliste*, Bowles's *The Sheltering Sky*', *New Comparison*, 31, (2001), p. 157.

The Abject Narrative in Simone de Beauvoir's
Le Sang des autres

Joanna Shearer
Oxford Brookes University

Sin originated with woman and because of her we all perish
-Ecclesiasticus

The notion of the impure and unclean female is not a recent construct. The taboos concerning pollution by adult female bodies have been frequently reiterated by many societies and their writers, so it is not surprising that many second-wave feminists took up 'the gendered female body' as a major source of oppression for women. Simone de Beauvoir famously wrote in *Le Deuxième Sexe,* 'On ne naît pas femme: on le devient'[1] thereby underlining the ways in which women's and men's bodies are differently and unequally imbued with social meanings. According to Barbara Brook, many feminist writers of the 1970s followed Beauvoir's lead 'in concentrating on the cultural formations of femininity and either ignoring their own potential to be pregnant bodies, or minimizing, as far as possible, the impact of pregnancy'.[2] The female body was rejected by women and seen as a negative, abject form. They saw it as 'shapeless, monstrous, damp, and slimy'; 'an area associated with change and the uncanny, and thus the occasion of fear and revulsion'.[3] However, later feminist writers who examined the liminal state of abjection attempted to re-appropriate the term so that it could be used in a positive, defining manner.

This study concerns a close reading of a scene in Simone de Beauvoir's *Le Sang des autres*, underpinned by the theorist Julia Kristeva's optimistic elaboration on the notion of the abject. Simone de Beauvoir is often accused of being incredibly harsh towards her female characters, but in the light of Kristevan theory the female protagonist in *Le Sang des autres* appears to have more strength than other critics have allowed for.

In order to undertake a Kristevan reading of Beauvoir, it is first necessary to fully understand the notion of abjection as defined in relation to women in accordance with Kristeva's text, *Pouvoirs de l'horreur*. This text is not at all straightforward, and a close reading is necessary to understand the gradual evolution of ideas. The second section of this study will examine Simone de Beauvoir, her uneasy relationship with female biology and how this comes out in her writing of an 'abject' narrative. In section three, I will undertake a close reading of *Le Sang des autres,* exploring the passages in which abjection serves as an identifying characteristic of the female protagonist and thus differentiates her from the patriarchal environment in which she lives.

I PLACING THE FEMALE IN ABJECTION

Defining abjection in *Pouvoirs de l'horreur* is a difficult task. Kristeva states that 'Toute sécrétion, épanchement, tout ce qui s'échappe du corps féminin ou masculin, souille'.[4] She classifies these secretions as abject because they disturb identity, system and order by blurring the boundaries between the inside and outside of the human body (p 12). Abjection is a menacing process; although we may desire to distance ourselves from the horror of abjection, it is impossible because this menace stems from the internal. Kristeva explains, 'A l'opposé de ce qui entre dans la bouche et nourrit, ce qui sort du corps, de ses pores et de ses orifices, marque l'infinitude du corps propre et suscite l'abjection' (p. 126-27). Abject substances such as vomit, excrement and menstrual blood emerge from our bodies because they are not needed. It may appear that abjection is a negative process, for it is based on expulsion. Kristeva writes that '[l]'abjection de soi serait la forme culminante de cette expérience du sujet auquel est dévoilé que tous ses objets ne reposent que sur la *perte* inaugurale fondant son être propre' (p. 12). This introduces the link between abjection and the mother and thus establishes the compelling connection between abjection and the female. Kristeva once stated in an interview that 'the relation to abjection is finally rooted in the combat that every human being carries on with the mother. For in order to become autonomous, it is necessary that once cut the instinctual dyad of the mother and the child and that one becomes something other'.[5] This loss of the mother evidently is completely *necessary* in order for the individual to define him/herself as a separate being. Therefore, this loss is not a negative, but rather a positive event in the child's development.

Kristeva's theory focuses directly on the role of the archaic mother (the all-encompassing mother that is not fully separated from her child) in the child's development, for she feels that Freud concentrated too much on the 'murder of the father' taboo in his work, *Totem and Taboo*, and that he neglected to study the female image in-depth. She begs an answer to the question of how the confrontation with the feminine alters ideas about the development of the speaking subject and emphasizes the masculine/feminine division of language and corporeal control. Before the advent of language, the body's inside and outside are not completely distinguished. The outside is only understood by a projection from within the body; the only experiences that are known are pleasure and pain. Language names and distinguishes all the outside forces that act on the body.[6] However, Kristeva characterizes language as a masculine practice and thereby argues that it represses the feminine, which was before expressed by the body (previously defined by Kristeva as the domain of the female). Women's corporeal control is a very clearly defined female trait, and the power women have over the body is evidenced very early on by young children. Maternal authority is also first experienced as sphincteral training, and by this authority, the mother is thereby decreed the 'depositaire du corps propre'; she maps out the body for the child. However, when language is introduced, a separation occurs and represses the maternal authority and the corporeal mapping.[7] This process, though necessary to the child's development, is simply another demonstration of the patriarchal society's desire to emphasize the masculine traits so that the female strengths thus appear unnatural. However, in highlighting this split, Kristeva illuminates for many females their intrinsic powers, and although she states nothing directly, there is a certain amount of pride in the abject functions of the female body; functions that are not understood and in fact cause fear and jealousy in the eyes of the male population.

FEAR OF MOTHERS

The history of mother-phobia in many societies stresses the prevalent desire of males to suppress female power. In many of the anthropological studies in *Pouvoirs de l'horreur*, it is revealed that there exists a generalized fear of the female, particularly the mother. Kristeva theorizes that 'mothers are perhaps considered powerful because of pregnancy, the care they give their newborn infants, and the substantial role they play in their children's upbringing'. They 'exert the primary influence over an individual's development'.[8] Females are thus the shapers of the next generation. Jealousy by the male of the female functions may also be a founding reason for this fear. Kristeva states, 'There is a sort of rage against mothers; it is not only because they take care of the child, but because they carry it in their bodies. Man cannot do this,' She theorizes that 'it is here that certain desire is rooted, a certain negative desire, a certain rejection of the maternal function—a fascinated rejection'.[9] The female body is an object of mystery veiled in horror, and as with many unknown entities, it becomes synonymous with evil.

POLLUTION BY THE FEMALE

Although 'abject' substances are said to originate from both sexes, the female appears to be responsible for the pollution to society caused by abjection. In many societies, abjection is labelled as filth and is thus considered dangerous because it signifies the frailty of the human order.[10] This fear is a societal construct linked to prohibition and probably propagated by the male because of his fear and loathing of the mother. In many cases, women are blamed for creating this filth and even though these women are often passive members of society, they are considered to have great power that the men wish to suppress. Women are though to be the sources of the two main polluting objects (excrement and menstrual blood) and, as previously noted, these pose a danger to the order of society. Menstrual blood, the danger from within the body, makes clear the sexual differences between men and women and is therefore threatening to societal order. Excrement, the danger from outside the body, is associated with the feminine because it exits through an opening that small children might imagine the female sex organ to resemble (p. 86). There is also an element of impurity associated with the maternal function that originated in the Old Testament. In Leviticus, it reads, 'Because of her parturition and the blood that goes with it, she will be impure: according to the separation for her infirmity, shall she be unclean' (12:2). Kristeva accepts that 'les termes d'impureté et de souillure [...] se trouvent attribués ici à la mère et en général aux femmes'. Menses and childbirth, Kristeva passively concludes, are a sign of the abomination provoked by the fertile feminine body (p. 119).

THE BIRTH-GIVING SCENE

In describing a text by Celine, Kristeva discusses the epitome of abjection—the birthgiving scene. 'La scène des scènes est ici non pas la scène dite primitive, mais celle de l'accouchement, inceste à l'envers, identité écorchée. L'accouchement: summum du carnage et de la vie, point brûlant de l'hésitation (dedans/dehors, moi/autre, vie/mort), horreur et beauté, sexualité et négation brutale du sexuel' (p. 181). This process is also described as an 'acte d'expulsion violente par laquelle le corps naissant s'arrache aux substances de l'intérieur maternel' (p. 120). Is the female's most intense, passionate and extreme moment thus reduced to a description of the abject matter that is involved in the process, or is the brutal creation of a new identity through the apparent diligence of a single sex the ultimate focus? The pain and terror are all focused on one being at this point, and it is not yet the subject who occupies the spotlight. The abject matter that results merely underlines the difficult role of the female (and the physical and mental pain she endures) in the life-giving process. It is clear that in the search for self-identity, Kristeva regards childbirth as a defining moment for both mother and child.

II READING SIMONE DE BEAUVOIR AS 'UN ÉCRIVAIN DE L'ABJECT'

Kristeva writes that a narrative is 'la tentative la plus élaborée [...] de situer un être parlant entre ses désirs et leurs interdits, bref à l'intérieur du triangle oedipien' (p.165). This task is arguably rather simple for Simone de Beauvoir. Her fiction, it has been claimed, merely amounts to the description of various events and states of emotion from her own life-history. This widespread opinion was first introduced by Jean-Raymond Audet in *Simone de Beauvoir face à la mort.* He insisted that all of Beauvoir's fictional characters (but particularly the female ones) are Beauvoir herself, and she endows them 'with all the vicissitudes of her own psychological, sociological and political development'.[11] Thus, if we take Audet's view, Beauvoir's personal journey as the female in the disturbing Oedipal triangle can be understood as being chronicled in her novels. In working through her difficult emotions on paper, it is possible that she was able to explore some of her own questions about the female body, a practice that is discussed by Kristeva. Anna Smith notes Kristeva's view of writing as a form of feminine therapy: 'Kristeva believes that the profound ambiguity of abjection is at its most relentless in literature, which manages at the same time to provide some sort of cathartic relief through sublimation'.[12] Smith elaborates: 'The woman who approaches abjection through writing inhabits it differently, improperly perhaps. Never fully at home in the body, nor fully at ease within signs, the writer's body...is (seemingly) her text'. [13]   Writing therefore becomes the incorporation of body and language into one instrument. It succeeds in finding an outlet for a female's self-expression, and may, writes Smith, 'absorb our terror, our aggression, and our disappointment'.[14] Kristeva clearly shares this view, as she once remarked in an interview, 'It's necessary to see how all the great works of art ... [are] masterful sublimations of those crises of subjectivity which are known, in another connection, as psychotic crises.' [15]

Beauvoir is well-known for her body-loathing and is fascinated by the female body's abject functions in many of her texts. In *Le Deuxième Sexe*, she states that menstruation makes a woman feel that her body is 'une chose opaque aliénée'.[16]   Throughout this supposedly feminist work (which logically should be empowering women), the female body is characterized as a mere vehicle for childbirth and Beauvoir states that a female's reproductive cycle has a great effect on everyday life. Motherhood, for Beauvoir, is not a pleasant role but conversely a binding duty that is restrictive and defining; freedom of the female is irrevocably lost. Beauvoir also detests the thought of her own body ageing in any way. The emphasis that she places on the body of Hélène, her young female protagonist in *Le Sang des autres*, is therefore all the greater as we realize the purity that is symbolically expressed by her youthful appearance and childlike mannerisms. As is the norm in Beauvoir's texts, the main female character is treated in a very harsh manner as she struggles to find her role in life and overcome her problems of femininity and identity.

III THE NOTION OF ABJECTION IN *LE SANG DES AUTRES*

Fear of abject substances, woman's polluting power, the horror of childbirth and mimesis of an archaic 'other' are all themes that enter Simone de Beauvoir's novel, *Le Sang des autres*. The title itself encourages an abject reading from the point of view of the eternal other, the female. However, the text is not easily categorized as a 'feminist' novel, and just as one must struggle in Kristeva's theories to find a positive reading of the feminine and the maternal, one must be equally astute in criticizing Beauvoir's novel. Although Beauvoir implies in *The Second Sex* that she prefers to ignore her own body as a signifier, she appears to emphasize the body of her protagonist in this 1945 work.

Le Sang des autres revolves around the main characters' search for identity. Hélène, the female protagonist, wrestles hopelessly with feelings of inadequacy and searches anxiously for someone to emulate; a substitute archaic mother. Kristeva defines this concept of 'mimesis' as a desire to become homologous to another in order to become oneself.[17] The 'childlike' Hélène echoes a pattern that normally occurs in the pre-oedipal stage, but her pairing is carefully calculated, and unlike the forced pairing of mother and child, Hélène carefully chooses her lover/mentor Jean Blomart because of his strength, a quality she covets. Hélène consequently attempts to form her own gender role by transcending the female body and imitating male characteristics. In this manner she may establish a border between herself and the weak female she perceives herself to be. By falling under the spell of male domination, Hélène almost seems to oppress herself.

Jean, meanwhile, is portrayed by Hélène as divine rather than merely masculine. She views Jean as a God-like figure and remarks that he seems to have no desires and no needs. It seems impossible to her that this completely autonomous man could have once been linked to an archaic mother. 'C'était si drôle de penser qu'il devait la vie à quelqu'un'.[18] Interestingly enough, Hélène appears to be autonomous to Jean:

> Toi, tu n'étais pas dans mes bras un corps abandonné, mais une femme tout entière. Tu me souriais bien en face, pour que je sache que tu étais là, librement, que tu n'étais pas perdue dans le tumulte de ton sang. Tu ne te sentais pas la proie d'une fatalité honteuse; au milieu des élans les plus passionnés, quelque chose dans ta voix, dans ton sourire disait: 'C'est parce que j'y consens'.[19]

It is perhaps her feeble attempts at masculinity mimesis that form his positive judgement of her. Hélène, though, swears that she cannot live without Jean. 'Tu ne te rends pas compte de ce que j'ai vécu pendant ce mois, tu ne peux pas te rendre compte. C'était, c'était abject.'[20] Hélène's use of the term abject is meant to denote a state of nothingness and horror. Without Jean's presence, her false self cannot persist and she falls back into her role as the undefined eternal other.

Hélène has not yet accepted the notion that abjection is a physical state or realized that abject substances will aid in self-definition.

Hélène's search for identity leads her to the maternal role. Hélène, perhaps subconsciously, sets out to prove herself capable of fulfilling a female's proper duties by becoming pregnant. When asked why she had the dangerous and random sexual encounter that brought about the pregnancy, she replies, 'Je voulais me venger'[21], perhaps suggesting that she wanted to prove everyone wrong who treated her as an ignorant child. Her resulting pregnancy, although unintentional, serves as an authentication of her journey into womanhood. Even though the goal of the passage is an abortion, the event is narrated as a birth. The abortionist plays the role of the physician and Jean tends to his duties as the imposter-father. The abortionist begins, 'ce n'est pas encore venu… Vous avez bien fait de m'appeller. Je vais vous aider. Ça sera tout de suite fini'. Hélène is required to 'Pousser fort' and afterwards, Jean is called to collect the bloody result. 'La cuvette était pleine de sang et dans cette crème rouge flottaient de gros morceaux de mou de veau'.[22] This horribly abject scene emphasizes the suffering and strength that every female must endure when introducing a new life into the world, but moreover, it recalls each female's own origins and her desires to separate herself from the archaic mother.

The passage that concerns the unborn child, though it describes only Hélène's pain, is written from the point of view of Jean. The entire novel is divided into alternating chapters from both Jean's and Hélène's perspective, but the division is hardly equal. His presence haunts many of her scenes, whereas she is not even mentioned in many of his. His narratives begin and end the novel, lending a patriarchal quality to the text. Negative female stereotypes enter the narrative and Jean's distaste for the female is emphasized in a short diatribe about the original 'rottenness', a term denoted by the French feminine gender:

> Parce que j'ai voulu me garder pur alors qu'*elle* [my emphasis] était installée en moi, mêlée à ma chair, à mon souffle, la pourriture originelle. Nous sommes vaincus; les hommes sont vaincus. À leur place proliférera sur la terre une race animale neuve; la palpitation aveugle de la vie ne se distinguera plus de la pourriture de la mort: la vie se gonfle et se défait d'un rythme égal, muscles, sang, sperme, et grouillement de vers repus.[23]

The fear of the power of the female to defile and eventually decimate society by her filth permeates the text. The female body is repeatedly used as a source of horror and danger.

Hélène is classified alternatively as child and woman in the text and throughout the beginning of the abject abortion passage Hélène is still viewed by Jean as innocently childlike. Her 'paternal' lover is amazed that 'sous sa peau enfantine', a baby exists. He muses, 'Je l'avais traitée comme une enfant capricieuse; c'était une si petite fille. Et déja son corps connaissait cette souffrance aigüe de femme'.[24] There are therefore two child-like subjects within this portion of the text. However, Hélène's role as the subject is treated as if it may come to an end; she begins to take on the miserable task of becoming the object as the centrepiece of the passage becomes the unborn foetus. Kristeva writes that 'l'enfant peut servir d'indice à sa mère pour son authentification à elle, il n'y a guère de raison qu'elle lui serve d'intermédiaire afin qu'il s'autonomise et s'authentifie à son tour'.[25] The mother's body is thus classified as a useless receptacle after she has housed another life in her 'natural mansion'. Hélène had been searching for a workable definition of her own female identity, but instead she discovered an unequal relationship to an 'other'. It is at this point that Hélène realizes that instead of questioning the notion of 'otherness', she should have been searching for identity within herself.

The blood referenced in the title of the novel may be intended to denote that of the soldiers involved in the Second World War, but if it is taken to represent the defiling blood of the female, a new reading of the text may result. According to Kristeva, all blood is impure because it reminds one of the 'tendance au meurtre [du père] dont l'homme doit se purger. Mais cet élément vital qu'est le sang réfère aussi aux femmes, à la fertilité, à la promesse de fécondation. Il devient alors un carrefour sémantique fascinant, lieu propice de l'abjection où *mort* et *féminité*, *meurtre* et *procréation, arrêt de vie* et *vitalité,* vont se rejoindre.[26] Eventually, in Hélène's journey into female adulthood, we see her blood transformed in Jean's mind into a filthy substance that serves only to pollute and defile. The child Hélène carries is a being 'qu'elle nourrissait avec son sang'[27], the same way one might describe the maggots that feed on a corpse. Later, Beauvoir writes, 'Et voilà, qu'elle était couchée là, dans son sang rouge de femme, et sa jeunesse et sa gaieté s'écoulaient de son ventre avec un gargouillement obscène'. [28] This passage appears to reference a girl's first menses and the horror and fascination expressed by male society towards the abject functions of the female productive system.

Hélène's path towards self-discovery actually begins in this horrific abortion scene. Hélène recognizes herself existing because of her abject fluids. Kristeva emphasizes the positive self-identifying qualities of every woman's abjection in the introductory chapter of *Pouvoirs de l'horreur*. 'Ces humeurs, cette souillure, cette merde sont ce que la vie supporte à peine et avec peine de la mort. J'y suis aux limites de ma condition de vivant. De ces limites se dégage mon corps comme vivant'. [29] Hélène also finds comfort in her body's ability to exclude substances. When she vomits, she notes, 'Il y avait à ses pieds une espèce de pâté blanchâtre, mais personne n'y prenait garde. "Comme si on ne pouvait même plus avoir honte de son corps", pensa-t-elle. "comme si même mon corps n'était plus moi"'. [30] A bit later, '[e]lle reconnaissait cette longue plainte de son coeur et le goût de sa salive dans sa bouche. "C'est moi. C'est bien moi"'. [31] These two contrasting quotations represent the founding problematics of the text. Should females be content to be represented by the body or not? The female protagonist appears to come to terms with her own body and her autonomy results from the comfort she finds in that internal relationship. Hélène affirms: 'Je suis vivante. Je serai toujours vivante. Elle sentait sa vie qui battait dans sa poitrine et cet instant était éternel.' [32] Beauvoir appears, briefly, to place some positive, identifying value in the female body.

The text, although it had appeared to be leaning towards the slant of feminism, becomes problematic at this point as Hélène is literally destroyed so that Jean may form his personal philosophy of being-for-others. The eternal other, the female, therefore sheds her blood a second time in a sacrifice to the male, the apparent ultimate intellectual and physical authority of the text. At times throughout the narrative, Hélène does appear to have found strength in solitude. Yet even when Hélène feels at peace with herself, she likens the feeling to a time when she had a paternal other watching over her. Just before her death, Hélène feels 'légère et comblée comme aux plus beaux soirs de son enfance, quand elle reposait dans les bras d'un Dieu paternel'. [33]

Conclusion

Julia Kristeva's theories concerning the female body's pollution of society may initially be read as negative impressions of female body-loathing, but upon closer inspection her ideas of self-identification appear to place great worth in the female body throughout each woman's personal, intellectual and social evolution. Similarly, Beauvoir appears to begin to allow her female protagonist in *Le Sang des autres* the opportunity to come to terms with the positive aspects of her abject body, but unfortunately Beauvoir kills Hélène off before she has a chance to fully explore these ideas. It must be noted, however, that this 1945 work was a very early attempt to re-appropriate the female body's abject functions in anything resembling a positive manner, and since Beauvoir's time, the discussion concerning the abject female body has become overwhelmingly favourable. Recent attempts have been made by writers such as Annie Leclerc, Chantal Chawaf and Marie Darrieusecq to find their own body discourse and to break out of the trap of abjection. Beauvoir's early attempts to recuperate the body as a space for the articulation of female identity should not be overlooked as she furnished many writers of future generations, including Kristeva, with a host of conjectures either to refute or to enhance.

NOTES

[1] Simone de Beauvoir, *Le Deuxième Sexe II: L'Expérience vécue* (Gallimard, 1949), p. 13.
[2] Barbara Brook, *Feminist Perspectives on the Body* (Pearson Education Ltd., 1999), p. 6.
[3] Brook, p. 158.
[4] Julia Kristeva, *Pouvoirs de l'horreur* (Editions du Seuil, 1980), p.121.
[5] Ross Mitchell Guberman (ed.), *Julia Kristeva Interviews* (Columbia University Press,1996), p. 118.
[6] *Pouvoirs de l'horreur*, pp. 73-76.
[7] *Pouvoirs de l'horreur*, pp. 86-87.
[8] Guberman, p. 72.
[9] Guberman, p. 118.
[10] *Pouvoirs de l'horreur*, p. 86. All further notes to this work will be referenced in the text.
[11] Jean-Raymond Audet, *Simone de Beauvoir face à la mort* (Editions l'Age d'Homme, 1979), p. 91.
[12] Smith, p. 151.

13 Smith, p. 160.

14 Smith, p. 152.

15 Guberman, p. 16.

16 Simone de Beauvoir, *Le Deuxième Sexe I* (Gallimard, 1949), p. 67.

17 *Pouvoirs de l'horreur*, p. 20.

18 Simone de Beauvoir. *Le Sang des autres* (Éditions Gallimard, 1945), p. 174.

19 *Le Sang des autres*, p. 137.

20 *Le Sang des autres*, p. 235.

21 *Le Sang des autres*, p. 126.

22 *Le Sang des autres,* pp. 130-31.

23 *Le Sang des autres*, p.238.

24 *Le Sang des autres*, pp.125-26.

25 *Pouvoirs de l'horreur*, p. 20.

26 *Pouvoirs de l'horreur*, p. 116.

27 *Le Sang des autres*, p. 125

28 *Le Sang des autres*, p. 129

29 *Pouvoirs de l'horreur*, p. 11.

30 *Le Sang des autres*, p. 263.

31 *Le Sang des autres*, p. 276.

32 *Le Sang des autres*, p.301.

33 *Le Sang des autres*, p. 301.

Cross-dressing and the Transgression of Cultural and Sexual Taboos in the Works of Pierre Loti

Peter Turberfield
University of Reading

The famous "Orientalist" writer Pierre Loti (1850-1923) is renowned for his enthusiastic penchant for dressing-up, a predilection which continued even after he achieved the full rank of ship's captain in the navy.[1] As well as adopting various "Oriental" disguises when abroad, he also indulged his passion at home, notoriously introducing himself to Sarah Bernhardt 'wrapped in a carpet like Cleopatra before Caesar.'[2] He actually seemed to invite ridicule as is revealed in his friend Léon Daudet's malicious remark: 'Nous disions de lui qu'il mettait un masque pour aller acheter un croissant.'[3] Whilst such behaviour might have appeared childish to many of his contemporaries, it can conversely be interpreted as being of central importance to an understanding of the image he projects. His deliberate flouting of dress codes, and implicitly of the hierarchical relationships of social class or military rank that were embodied in them, was deeply disturbing or even offensive to those around him. This is noted by Alain Buisine who comments that 'il y a quelque chose de fondamentalement indécent, inacceptable même, dans sa conduite vestimentaire' (Buisine, L'écrivain, p. 96). Buisine locates the cause of this discomfort: 'La société pardonne rarement à ceux qui se jouent systématiquement du vêtement car elle n'ignore pas qu'une certaine stabilité des codes vestimentaires favorise le maintien de ses structures'. He continues by putting Loti's adoption of costume into this context: 'les plaisanteries d'un Pierre Loti [...] finissent par gêner aux entournures. Ses connaissances trouvent-elles finalement si drôle que cela de ne jamais savoir dans quelle tenue il va débarquer chez elles, parfois accompagné d'un acolyte dont elles ignorent s'il est matelot de deuxième classe ou officier supérieur?' (Buisine, L'écrivain, pp. 96-97). Loti was obviously very much aware of the effect he was causing, enjoying the uncertainty and questioning of identity that his transgressive disguises created. Whether interpreted as mere jokes or as a more serious attack on the hierarchies of his social milieu, the disturbing effect of his crossing of class borders is undeniable. His parallel adoption of "Oriental" garb and the similarly implicit crossing of cultural borders was of course equally disquieting, calling into question not only social but also the forbidden territory of cultural/racial boundaries.

Inseparable from Loti's cross-dressing is his portrayal and experience of "exotic sex", that evocation of eroticism that seems to epitomize representations of the "Orient" in Western imagination. Similar to the pleasure he obviously takes in flouting dress-codes is the evident delight he takes in his scandalous subject matter. Although ostensibly heterosexual, Loti's portrayal of liaisons with what were basically a string of "Oriental" prostitutes produced an obviously desired shocked reaction, one epitomized by Edmond and Jules de Goncourts' notorious dismissal of his work in their comment that '[il] n'a fait au fond que chanter, tout au long de ses œuvres, les prostituées qui font le trottoir sous les cocotiers' (Buisine, L'écrivain, p. 32).[4] The provocative nature of his accounts is inevitably increased given their at times only thinly veiled homoeroticism, both in the accounts of his close "friendships" with "Oriental" men and boys and in those which detail his fascination with the sailors with whom he served. Far from being cause for contemptuous dismissal as the Goncourt brothers suggest, however, this exploration of forbidden sexual experience is of central importance to an understanding of the underlying themes of Loti's work. The idea of the "exotic sex" available in the "Orient", of 'a different type of sexuality, perhaps more libertine and less guilt-ridden', as Edward Said puts it, has of course its parallel in the "exotic sex" available closer to home in cross-class relations.[5] Christopher Robinson outlines the representation of this variation on exotic sex in nineteenth-century literature, describing it as characterized by 'a fascination with the otherness represented by young working class masculinity'.[6] Just as in the "Oriental" version of "exotic sex", "otherness" is the key to arousal: 'the frisson comes in part from the very existence of the gulf; they have no desire to eliminate it' (Robinson, Scandal, p. 47). Class difference is in this way similar to racial/cultural difference in providing a sense of escape, and its essence as difference, in recognizing a border that must be crossed, is an essential part of the transgressive pleasure it affords. Whilst such "exotic sex" explores "otherness" and taboos such as homosexuality, seemingly embodying a rejection of the accepted norms of the protagonist's social/cultural background, an enjoyment of the exotic experience demands this same background as something to transgress against. Marjorie Garber summarizes this paradox by saying that it is 'precisely upon transgression, upon the sensation or perception of daring, of breaking a law or flaunting [*sic*] a taboo' that much eroticism depends.[7] Loti's cross-dressing and interlinked sexual experience may undermine certain social "norms", yet simultaneously requires them for the indispensable role they play in his forbidden fantasies.

Roland Barthes argues that clothing, for 'ce fanatique du travestisme', represents an identification with "Otherness", an essence that for Loti, in the "Oriental" context, means an "Orient" 'désancré de l'Occident et du modernisme'.[8] His identity is in this way composed of a stereotypical image of the "Orient" that his clothes attempt to reproduce. It is this link between Loti's cultural cross-dressing and the western stereotypical concept of the "Orient" that offers a key to an understanding of his work. The transvestite's clothing functions in a similar way to the colonial stereotype of the "Orient" in veiling difference whilst simultaneously exaggerating it. The ambiguity of Loti's sense of cultural identity is expressed in his stereotypical disguise, a disguise which plays an essential role in his experience of "exotic" and equally ambiguous sexuality. Ideas of colonial oppression and sexual oppression are in this way linked in Loti's work, illustrating Freud's idea that civilization 'behaves towards sexuality as a people does which has subjected another to its exploitation.'[9] Loti's transvestism thus assumes a special importance in the role it plays in the transgression of cultural and sexual taboos. A closer analysis of the nature of his sexuality reveals the full implications of his transgressive behaviour.

In his essay 'On Narcissism: An Introduction' Freud discusses a link between homosexuality and narcissism, and notes that some homosexuals 'in their [...] choice of love-objects [...] have taken as a model not their mother but their own selves.'[10] In other words '[they] are plainly seeking *themselves* as a love-object, and are exhibiting a type of object-choice which must be termed "narcissistic".' He outlines the variations of possible narcissistic object-choice:

> A person may love:-
> (1) According to the narcissistic type:
>   (a) what he himself is (i.e. himself),
>   (b) what he himself was,
>   (c) what he himself would like to be,

(d) someone who was once part of himself. (SE14, p. 90)

These basic patterns of object-choice provide the basis for three different models of male homosexuality, outlined by Kaja Silverman.[11] The basis of the third model of male homosexuality that Silverman details is to be found in a footnote that Freud added to the English translation of 'Three Essays on Sexuality' in 1910.[12] He writes that 'future inverts, in the earliest years of their childhood, pass through a phase of very intense but short-lived fixation to a woman (usually their mother), and that, after leaving this behind, they identify themselves with a woman and take *themselves* as their sexual object.' This means they 'proceed from a narcissistic basis, and look for a young man who resembles themselves and whom *they* may love as their mother loved *them*.' They are also 'by no means insensible to the charms of women, but have continually transposed the excitation aroused by women onto a male object.' This third model is developed by Freud in his analysis 'Leonardo da Vinci and a Memory of His Childhood':

> The boy represses his love for his mother: he puts himself in her place, identifies himself with her, and takes his own person as a model in whose likeness he chooses the new objects of his love [...] the boys whom he now loves as he grows up are [...] only substitutive figures and revivals of himself in childhood – boys whom he loves in the way in which his mother loved *him* when he was a child.[13]

Silverman shows how the Leonardo model is complicated by the interpretation of a passage taken from one of Leonardo's notebooks in which he 'cites as one of his earliest and most formative memories the experience of being visited in his cradle by a bird who opened his mouth, and struck him repeatedly on the mouth with its tail' (Silverman, *Male*, p. 369). This is taken by Freud as a 'memory [that] was a fantasy dating from a later moment, subsequently transposed onto infancy'. Freud shows that as the tail 'is one of the most familiar symbols and substitutive expressions for the male organ', 'the situation in the phantasy, of a vulture opening the child's mouth and beating about inside it vigorously with its tail, corresponds to the idea of an act of *fellatio*' (SE11, pp. 85-86). Silverman proposes that this requires 'the desiring subject of the

Leonardo fantasmatic be understood to occupy the position of the vulture or kite, i.e. of the *active* mother' (Silverman, *Male*, p. 370). She is however putting this position forward in direct contradiction to Freud's reading of the scene as a *'passive* fantasy' with its 'erotic center [coinciding] with the position of the child'. The suggestion is that there are 'two possible love-objects' that the desiring subject is 'capable of moving between an active and a passive position.' Silverman shows that if this is the case and there are 'two possible positions in the vulture fantasmatic, in order for each of them to emerge as the site of the love object it must have been possible for Leonardo as subject to occupy at least temporarily the position of the other, and hence to move back and forth between an identification with the mother, and an identification with his own youth' (Silverman, *Male*, pp. 370-71). She accordingly proposes two diagrams for her third paradigm:

Paradigm 3 (The Leonardo Model)

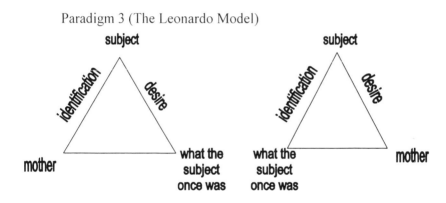

The idea of 'reversibility' is emphasized in this model. Silverman stresses that it is 'not merely a palimpsest, in which identification with the mother is inscribed over the more archaic text of desire for her, but a constant oscillation between these two modalities' (Silverman, *Male*, p. 371).

The reversibility of this third libidinal paradigm is seen as making it extremely 'volatile' as 'desire for the (phallic) [i.e. pre-Oedipal, non-castrated] mother implies occupying the passive or receptive position of the child in the Leonardo fantasmatic, whereas identification with her necessitates occupying instead the active or insertive position of the vulture or kite and [...] both are perpetually operative' (Silverman, *Male*,

p. 371). Both positions within this vulture fantasmatic are noted as '[marking] out the mouth as the ideal locus for the penis' (Silverman, *Male*, p. 372). This 'attests to the centrality of the mother, for the mouth represents a privileged site of maternal care.' The desiring subject, through the reversibility of the paradigm, is enabled 'both to commemorate his earlier love for the mother by experiencing pleasure at the site of that erotogenic zone, as he did when he was a child, and to dramatize his subsequent identification with her by inserting his penis between the lips of the love-object.' Both positions here 'dramatically [reconceive] identification with the mother' as '[maternal] identification [...] depends upon none of the usual tropes of femininity, with the single exception of those that hinge directly on motherhood.' For Silverman 'it signifies neither receptivity, exhibitionism, passivity, nor masochism, but rather *activity* and *penetration*', because in this model 'it is only from the maternal position that one wields the penis.' Such a 'radically revisionary inscription of femininity' is explained through denial of the castration crisis: 'identification with the mother functions as a mechanism for disavowing [the revelation of anatomical difference], i.e. by refusing to acknowledge her penile "lack"'. In other words '[by] incorporating the mother, the homosexual subject is able to make good her anatomical "deficiency"; in effect, he provides the missing organ through his own body.' This is of course a form of fetishism, in Silverman's words a 'peculiar fetishism, which covers over the absence of a penis with the penis itself'.

The implications of this fetishism are two-fold. It can be seen as 'the inability of the homosexual subject to assimilate the anatomical particularity of the mother – as a stubborn refusal of alterity' or in more political terms as 'a resistance to the whole process of devaluation which is made to follow from woman's "difference" – as a refusal to accede to the equation of the mother with insufficiency' (Silverman, *Male*, p. 372). This refusal is made all the more emphatic in 'the dramatic exclusion of the father from the Leonardo model of homosexuality.' The model in this way 'works even more definitively against Oedipal normalisation than does the negative Oedipal complex' as it 'not only defies the rule of paternal succession, but it situates the father altogether outside the fields of desire and identification' (Silverman, *Male*, p. 373). This leads to the conclusion that 'although the subject of the Leonardo model of homosexuality is unable to relinquish his demand for the penis, and incapable of either loving or identifying with the mother except through relation to it, that organ functions not as a marker of symbolic privilege and the Law, but rather as an erotically resonant organ.' As 'it remains unauthorized by the Name-of-the-Father, the penis is able to circulate freely between desiring subject and desired object, and even to function as an imaginary appendage to the mother.'

It is Silverman's third model which would appear to be the most closely matched to the sexuality revealed in Loti's work. In every situation in which he portrays a sexual relationship with a woman, there is always a strong suggestion of a parallel and indeed more intense passion for a man. This would seem to follow the pattern of 'reversibility' Silverman develops from Freud. The male objects are invariably youths and in some way under "Loti's" protective wing. They may in this sense be seen as 'substitutive figures and revivals of himself in childhood'. Following Freud's model of narcissistic object-choice, "Loti" seems to desire not only 'what he once was', but also in his imagination 'what he himself would like to be'. The male objects of "Loti's" desire are accordingly psychologically childlike, representing himself as a child, yet emphasis is also placed on their physical perfection, his own lack of which Loti acutely regretted. These qualities that are necessary for the narcissistic "Loti", who has 'taken [himself] as love-object', are perfectly reproduced in the person of Yves. Yves is the name Loti gives in his published work to the character he bases on a sailor friend Pierre Le Cor. It was with Pierre that Loti enjoyed dressing as a common sailor and defying the conduct expected of a naval officer. Yves/Pierre is the picture of physical perfection: 'Quand Pierre enlève ses vêtements, on dirait une statue grecque, dépouillant son enveloppe grossière, et on l'admire. Dans le même albâtre bronzé, dur et poli, se dessinent les saillies mobiles des muscles, et les lignes puissantes de l'athlète antique.'[14] The real reason for the admiration Loti feels lies beyond the superficial level of the obvious physical attraction the description reveals. This is made clear in another entry in the *Journal intime* where "Loti" explains the reason for his friendship with Pierre and his fellow 'gabiers': 'ils sont ce que j'aurais le plus désiré être moi-même : il sont simples, primitifs et beaux. [...] Et puis surtout ils représentent à mes yeux la *jeunesse...*' (Loti, *Journal*, p. 96). In the primitive simplicity of their youth and physical beauty they represent both 'what ["Loti"] once was' and as he clearly states 'what he himself would like to be'. Another description of Yves taken from *Mon frère Yves* confirms "Loti's" fascination with this combination of strength and youth: 'Grand, maigre de la maigreur des antiques, avec les bras musculeux, le col et la carrure d'un athlète, l'ensemble du personnage donnant le sentiment de la force tranquille et légèrement dédaigneuse.'[15] This intimidating manly image is belied by his smile, which is equally lovingly described, and reveals the vulnerable child within: 'Figure immobile, marmoréenne, excepté dans les moments rares où paraît le sourire ; alors tout se transforme et on voit qu'Yves est très jeune. Le sourire de ceux qui ont souffert : il a une douceur d'enfant et illumine les traits durcis [...]'.

To further qualify Yves for his role as "Loti's" narcissistic object choice is "Loti's" position as his protector. He quite literally, at Yves' mother's request, assumes her position: 'la mère d'Yves me recommanda solennellement son fils, et cela resta toute la vie' (Loti, *Romans*, p. 413). "Loti" refers to Yves as 'son frère' but in the scene where he solemnly swears on the Cross to Yves' mother to look after him, he is obviously being given a more parental role. The childlike submission with which Yves accepts this transfer of protection also supports this interpretation:

> Et puis je pris la main d'Yves, qui baissait la tête, rêveur :
> - Et toi, tu m'obéiras, tu me suivras... *mon frère ?*
> Lui, répondit tout bas, hésitant, détournant les yeux, avec le sourire d'un enfant :
> - Mais oui... bien sûr... (Loti, *Romans*, p. 415)

This scene would appear to add to a very strong case for classifying "Loti's" object-choice of Yves as following the pattern of homo/bisexuals of the Leonardo model who 'proceed from a narcissistic basis, and look for a young man who resembles themselves and whom *they* may love as their mother loved *them.*'

It is also to be noted that Yves and the 'gabiers' are both Breton and of course from a different social background from the naval officer "Loti". As well as representing "Loti's" narcissistic object-choice, they can therefore also be seen as filling an "exotic" cross-class and cross-cultural role. Their combination of youth and the "exotic" is consequently parallel to that of "Loti's" other object-choices. In *Aziyadé* "Loti" clearly explains the reason for his attraction to his friends/lovers, in terms strikingly similar to those used to describe Yves and the 'gabiers'. He contrasts their youth with his own maturity, but emphasizes the rejuvenating effect they have on him:

> On déciderait difficilement quel est le plus enfant d'Achmet ou d'Aziyadé, ou même de Samuel. J'étais vieux et sceptique ; auprès d'eux, j'avais l'air de ces personnages de Buldwer qui vivaient dix vies humaines sans que les années pussent marquer sur leur visage, et logeaient une vieille âme fatiguée dans un jeune corps de vingt ans.
> Mais leur jeunesse rafraîchit mon cœur [...].[16]

The double positions that "Loti" describes here are again consistent with the double identification Silverman details in her version of the Leonardo paradigm. He is at once the older (and suggestively grammatically feminine) 'vieille âme fatiguée' and the (grammatically masculine) youth of 'le jeune corps de vingt ans', corresponding with the reversibility of identification with and desire for the mother and the subject as he once was.

The pattern of the Leonardo model also of course corresponds with the idyll of "Loti's" female-dominated childhood as portrayed in *Le Roman d'un enfant* and the intense love he felt for his mother and all of her substitutes, whom he describes fondly as 'les figures vénérées de tantes et de grands-mères qui ont entouré mon enfance'.[17] The exclusion of the father figure Silverman emphasizes is also particularly apposite. She stresses that the Leonardo model 'situates the father altogether outside the fields of desire and identification', and that therefore the penis 'functions not as a marker of symbolic privilege and the Law, but rather as an erotically resonant organ'. Again we can see the parallel that is suggested with Loti's own experience, as witness the virtual exclusion of his father from his writing, his eschewing of the family name Viaud, and his own later lack of interest in adopting the role of father to his own children, both legitimate and illegitimate, beyond the obviously narcissistic pride he took in self-replication. The pursuit of sexual gratification is perhaps one of the most dominant themes in Loti's work, but nowhere does the portrayal of this gratification give way to the feelings of responsibility inherent in the usual patriarchal models of being either a husband or a father. The penis, as Silverman suggests, also acts as a kind of fetish: through identification with his mother the subject 'provides the missing organ through his own body'. Silverman shows how this can be seen as 'a resistance to the whole process of devaluation [...] – as a refusal to accede to the equation of the mother with insufficiency'. The maternal dominance of "Loti's" childhood, extending to the conspicuous absence/exclusion of his father from his work would again appear to be consistent with this interpretation.

In Loti's case the asymmetries of the power structure implicit in the relationships he portrays would appear to be unambiguously present. As a Western man "Loti" is in an undeniably dominant position in relation to his preferred object-choices. As Gagnière summarizes they are typically of 'une autre couleur de peau, d'une situation inférieure à la sienne, d'une civilisation et d'une race différentes'.[18] "Loti's" position enables him to take full advantage of perceived racial and social superiority and, in spite of his protestations to the contrary, the charge of sexual exploitation is one which is difficult to refute. The pattern of involvement and inevitable abandonment, regardless of any physical or psychological consequences, clearly reveals this imbalance in his self-centred (ab)use of his "partners".

Whilst "Loti" can be seen in this context of colonialist white male-domination, it is also possible, however, to read quite radically different and even contradictory interpretations into the accounts of his sexual experiences. Whilst at the conscious level Loti is writing within the "Orientalist" tradition and confirming the traditional role of exploitation that might be expected of him, he is at the same time, in direct contradiction, albeit at the level of the unconscious, imparting an extremely radical model of sexuality and identification which undermines the very patriarchal power structure he appears to be epitomizing. In colonialist terms the exploitative male is in the position of patriarchal authority. He wields the phallus and the "Oriental" woman (or man) stands in the place of the penetrated mother figure. Through his selfish behaviour "Loti" would seem to be upholding this classical patriarchal structure of Western domination of the "Orient", but a consideration of the implications of his mother-identification and narcissistic sexual object-choice would on the contrary seem to place him in the position of the "Oriental" mother-figure himself, in Silverman's words denying the phallus 'as a marker of symbolic privilege and the Law'. His indulgence in exotic sex therefore becomes not a part of the system of patriarchal colonialism, but simply a libidinal experience of the penis 'as an erotically resonant organ', subverting the power structure from within which he is apparently writing. Within this reading the implications of "Loti's" fetishistic adoption of "Oriental" costume and identification with the colonial subject are quite radical if taken to their logical conclusion. In Silverman's model, '[by] incorporating the mother, the homosexual subject is able to make good her anatomical "deficiency", in effect, he provides the missing organ through his own body.' By extending this idea to the colonial context "Loti's" identification with the "Orient", as played out in the forbidden dressing-up of his cross-cultural transvestism, becomes a radical empowerment of the colonized subject. Silverman's model proposes the reversibility of identification and desire and she describes the different roles which are correspondingly implicit, that 'desire for the (phallic) [i.e. pre-Oedipal, non-castrated] mother implies occupying the passive or receptive position of the child in the Leonardo fantasmatic, whereas identification with her necessitates occupying instead the active or insertive position of the vulture'. The feminine identification therefore 'signifies neither receptivity, exhibitionism, passivity, nor masochism, but rather *activity* and *penetration*', and as such is indeed a 'radically revisionary inscription of femininity' as 'it is only from the maternal position that one wields the penis.' "Loti's" identification with/desire for the "Orient" in this way reverses the roles of colonial domination, a totally forbidden concept. Through the expression of his identification and desire he is accepting the subordinate position in his function as colonizer, and assuming the dominant position of the phallic-mother as colonized subject. As a result it becomes possible to see his fetishistic cross-cultural transvestism, his forbidden assumption of "Oriental" clothing and experience of forbidden sexuality, as part of a very 'radically revisionary' process. What appear to be straight-forward accounts of exploitative behaviour symbolically become the exact opposite. The 'peculiar fetishism' which Silverman describes, 'which covers over the absence of a penis with the penis itself' becomes an empowerment of the "Oriental" subject through what would appear to be contradictory acts of exploitation.

NOTES

[1] Pierre Loti is the pseudonym under which the naval officer Julian Viaud wrote. To avoid confusion over identity in the use of names Loti will henceforth be used to indicate the position of implied author/public persona, and "Loti" to designate his protagonist/narrator.

[2] Michael Lerner, *Pierre Loti* (Twayne, 1974), p. 47.

[3] This is a quotation taken from "Candide", January 3rd 1935, in Alain Buisine, *Pierre Loti: L'écrivain et son double* (Tallandier, 1998), p. 92.

[4] Buisine is quoting from Edmond et Jules de Goncourt, *Journal. Mémoires de la vie littéraire* (l'Imprimerie Nationale de Monaco, 1957), vol. XVIII [1891-2], p. 163.

[5] Edward W. Said, *Orientalism* (Vintage Books, 1979), p. 190.

[6] Christopher Robinson, *Scandal in the Ink* (Cassell, 1995), p. 44.

[7] Marjorie Garber, *Bisexuality and the Eroticism of Daily Life* (Routledge, 2000) [1995], p. 278.

[8] Roland Barthes, *Le Degré zéro de l'écriture ; suivi de Nouveaux essais critiques* (Seuil, 1972), p. 180.

[9] Sigmund Freud, 'Civilisation and its Discontents' ('Das Unbehagen in der Kultur') [1930], in *The Complete Psychological Works of Sigmund Freud*, (eds., and trans., James Strachey, Anna Freud, Alix Strachey, and Alan Tyson) Standard Edition 21 (1927-1931) (Hogarth Press, 1961), p. 104. (Following references to Freud are all taken from the Standard Edition which will be designated SE.)

[10] SE14, 'On Narcissism: An Introduction' ('Zur Einführung des Narzissmus') [1914], p. 88.

[11] Kaja Silverman, *Male Subjectivity at the Margins* (Routledge, 1992), pp. 339-88.

[12] SE7, 'Three Essays on Sexuality' ('Drei Abhandlungen zur Sexualtheorie') [1905], p. 145.

[13] SE11, 'Leonardo da Vinci and a Memory of His Childhood' ('Eine Kindheitserinnerung des Leonardo da Vinci') [1910], pp. 99-100.

[14] Pierre Loti, *Cette Eternelle Nostalgie: Journal intime*, eds. Bruno Vercier, Alain Quella-Villéger, and Guy Dugas (Table Ronde, 1997) [1878-1911], p. 34.

[15] Pierre Loti, *Mon frère Yves* [1883] in *Romans : Omnibus* (Presses de la Cité, 1989), p. 375.

[16] Pierre Loti (anonymous), *Aziyadé – Stamboul 1876-1877*, [1879], in *Romans : Omnibus*, pp. 80-81.

[17] Pierre Loti, *Le Roman d'un enfant* (Calmann-Lévy, 1936) [1890], p. 6.

[18] Claude Gagnière, 'Pierre Loti ou le désenchantement' in Pierre Loti, *Romans : Omnibus*, p. VIII.

Marginalization and Transgression in the Novels of Marguerite Duras, Patrick Modiano and Marie Darrieussecq

Morag Young
Oxford Brookes University

Introduction

The linked themes of marginalization and transgression are prominent in the novels of Duras, Modiano and Darrieussecq, where liminal states abound, a prominence which appears to me to be closely connected with the three authors' major preoccupation: the quest for identity. This search for self, which underlies the three writers' *oeuvre,* involves the creation of characters whose underlying sense of insecurity drives them to the borders of society and, at times, beyond these limits. Significantly, Duras, Modiano and Darrieussecq were themselves to some degree alienated from mainstream French society, Duras by virtue of her upbringing in French Indochina, Modiano because of his Jewishness together with his father's ambivalent role in the Occupation and Darrieussecq, who was born and brought up in the Basque country, because of her rift with her dysfunctional family. Additionally, both Duras and Darrieussecq perceived themselves, as woman, to be marginalized in a male-dominated society. It is therefore not surprising that this sense of alienation should persist in their novels, whose central characters invariably exhibit some degree of marginalization from society. Duras's exploration of identity in the context of female sexual desire occurs on the fringes of the conventional world, Modiano, in his search for self, enters the twilight world of the collaborator and Darrieussecq explores issues of feminine marginalization in the couple and the family. Figures who transgress social norms are also prominent in the novels of all three writers. Anne Desbaresdes, in *Moderato Cantabile* (Gallimard, 1958), moves from a comfortable existence as the wife of a rich industrialist into a murky world of violence and murder centred round a dockside café. Modiano's characters, who exist in a moral vacuum, are frequently involved in criminal activities. Darrieussecq portrays the abjection of a prostitute in *Truismes* (P.O.L., 1996) and the transgression of a wife who deserts her husband in *Le Mal de mer* (P.O.L., 1999). Thus all three authors, in their quest for identity, venture into the realm of the forbidden.

I now propose to examine in greater detail the significance of the themes of marginalization and transgression into each author's novels. There is an underlying connection between the two terms in that both encompass the idea of a limit or border. Transgression implies overstepping a boundary, which is nowadays normally conceived of as a legal limit, while marginalization refers to the relegation of an individual or group to a border zone. The relationship between marginalization and transgression is reciprocal: whereas marginalization usually precedes transgression, as when a person who has been pushed to the boundaries of society oversteps these limits, having nothing more to lose, the reverse may be the case, as when a hitherto respected member of society transgresses and is marginalized as a result. In the case of the recidivist, a spiral situation occurs, in which marginalization and transgression reinforce each other. After returning briefly to the root causes of each writer's alienation, I will consider the importance of these two themes, together with the significance of liminal spaces, in his/her novels as a whole.

The authors' sense of alienation

Born in French Indochina, Duras spent little time in France before the age of nineteen. After her widowed mother had fallen foul of the French authorities, the family lived on the fringes of colonial society. It is not surprising, therefore, that Duras's feelings towards her mother country were highly ambivalent: the narrator in the autobiographical novel *L'Amant de la Chine du Nord* (Gallimard, 1991) describes herself as: "première en français tout le temps partout et détestant la France, inconsolable du pays natal et de l'enfance" (p. 36), the native country referred being of course French Indochina. Later in life, she expressed her essential rootlessness when she declared: "Je ne suis née nulle part".[1] Whereas, as Christine Blot-Labarrère has observed,[2] Duras did gain some sense of Frenchness as a result of her involvement in World War II, she qualified this by her increasing identification with Jewish Holocaust victims, as evidenced in Aurélia Steiner (a short story from *Le Navire nuit*, Mercure de France, 1979) and *Yann Andréa Steiner* (P.O.L., 1992). Her unorthodox views on the couple, together with her Bohemian lifestyle, also placed her on the margins of French polite society.

Modiano's strong feelings of marginalization stem directly from his parents' status as aliens: his mother was Belgian and his father was a stateless Jew, whose involvement in the Black Market during the Occupation was a source of guilt and shame to his son. Modiano was neglected by both parents and his father deserted the family home when Modiano was a teenager.[3] Modiano has described himself as having: "ni terroir, ni racines",[4] a deficit which could only be made up on his part by a return to the period of the Occupation which he considers to be "ma préhistoire".[5] In doing so, he distanced himself from his own generation, who were out on the barricades in 1968, while Modiano was engaged in writing his first novel, *La Place de l'étoile* (Gallimard, 1968).

Born in France of French parents, Darrieussecq appears less marginalized than either Duras or Modiano. Like them, however, she came from a dysfunctional family which had been marked by tragedy.[6] Her parents' inability to articulate their feelings led to a sense of alienation in their daughter, who resolved to explore the "non-dit" at the heart of the family in her writing.[7] Boundary situations prevail in her novels and in her exploration of the changing role of women in the couple and the family, her avowed aim is to break new ground: "Toujours aller plus loin. Chercher la frontière. Essayer de la dépasser".[8]

This underlying sense of marginalization on the part of the three authors finds its expression in their novels, which share several common features. Firstly, their protagonists are solitary figures, who either operate outside normal social groupings or, if they are within them, feel estranged from their surroundings. Secondly, border zones feature prominently in their writing. Thirdly, there is a desire on the part of the protagonists to cross boundaries and a certain degree of fascination with criminal activities, in which they sometimes become involved. I now propose to examine each of these three common elements in turn in the novels of the three authors.

Marginalization

Duras's principal characters function on the fringes of normal social groupings. In her more autobiographical novels, *Un Barrage contre le Pacifique* (Gallimard, 1950), *L'Amant* (Éditions de Minuit, 1984) and *L'Amant de la Chine du Nord*, the central character is a rebellious teenager who defies her family and its social conventions. The family, headed by the dominant figure of the mother, who is eccentric to the point of madness, is already at loggerheads with the colonial authorities in French Indochina. Thus a double degree of alienation is present in the novels: the daughter from the mother and the mother from French colonial society. In *L'Amant*, the marginalization of both daughter and mother is reinforced by the fact that neither is named: the narrator/daughter is referred to as *je/elle,* while the mother is *ma/sa/la mère/elle.* Elsewhere, Duras's almost exclusively female protagonists adopt a radical stance which drives a wedge between them and conventional bourgeois society: Anne Desbaresdes, as we have seen, abandons the comfortable space provided by her rich factory-owning husband for a working class world dominated by uncertainty and violence; Lol V. Stein, in *Le Ravissement de Lol V. Stein* (Gallimard, 1964), while ostensibly leading a settled married life, exists in a private world dominated by the obsessive re-enactment of a previous highly-charged sexual encounter, which precludes any meaningful engagement with the bourgeois world around her. For Duras's characters, the exploration of personal issues concerning female sexual identity and desire occurs in a private space on the margins of society.

For Modiano's protagonists, who are nearly always male, the situation is slightly different. Cut off from a community in which they have no roots, they are condemned to wander in a limbo-like state until they can reconnect with their past. Significantly, the majority of Modiano's characters have foreign-sounding names or pseudonyms e.g. Pacheco, Deyckecaire, Stioppa de Djagoriew. There is a clear progression throughout Modiano's writing from the early statement of alienation in his first trilogy (*La Place de l'étoile, La Ronde de nuit* (Gallimard, 1969) and *Les Boulevards de ceinture* (Gallimard, 1972)), where his Jewish identity is explored in the context of the Occupation, through his middle period, set mainly in the 1960s, where the limbo-like state referred to above is prevalent, to the second trilogy (*Voyage de noces* (Gallimard, 1990), *Fleurs de ruine* (Seuil, 1991) and *Dora Bruder* (Gallimard, 1997)),[9] in which he returns to the Occupation and, by embracing witness literature in *Dora Bruder,* is able to reclaim his past, thus reducing his sense of isolation.

Darrieussecq, like Duras, portrays women and identifies strongly with female marginalization in the modern world. Her protagonists include a woman forced into prostitution and thus to the fringes of society (*Truismes*), a deserted wife who feels marginalized as a result of her husband's unexplained departure but who finally overcomes this sense of isolation (*Naissance des fantômes* (P.O.L., 1998)), a wife who herself deserts her family for a new life, thus defying bourgeois conventions (*Le Mal de mer*), and a family whose members retreat into their own private worlds as the result of a past tragedy which they are unable to come to terms with (*Bref séjour chez les vivants* (P.O.L., 2001)). Darrieussecq's refusal to give names to most of her female characters reinforces their marginality: in *Le Mal de mer*, they are all simply referred to as *elle*.

Liminal Spaces

Each of the three authors makes prominent use of liminal spaces in connection with the marginalization outlined above. For Duras, the sea and the forest predominate. References to the sea pervade her work: the sea is a threatening presence in *Un Barrage contre le Pacifique*, the sound of the sea, a metaphor for the escape from conventions, punctuates *Moderato Cantabile* and the sea is more explicitly associated with deviant sexuality in *La Maladie de la mort* (Éditions de Minuit, 1982). The theme of the sea voyage recurs regularly in Duras's writing, from the early novel *Le Marin de Gibraltar* (Gallimard, 1952), to one of her last works, *Emily L* (Éditions de Minuit,1987). The curiously-named town S. Tahla, where Lol V. Stein lives, exists outside any recognizable geographical setting and has overtones of the sea: *thalassa*. The wildness and lack of restraint symbolized by the sea in Duras's novels are paralleled in her use of the forest as embodying a space where primitive impulses still hold sway. This is the domain of madness, personified by the figure of the beggarwoman, who dominates *Le Vice-consul* and recurs throughout Duras's writing.

Modiano's liminal spaces differ from those of Duras in being safe havens rather than wild places. His characters, though strongly drawn to Paris, feel the need to escape over the borders from the menace which constantly threatens them. Switzerland features prominently as a place of safety, being neutral and close to France. It is clear, however, that the Switzerland described by Modiano's narrators is not so much a geographical entity as a mental space, where time stands still: the principal character in *Livret de famille* (Gallimard, 1977) describes himself in the following terms: "J'avais atteint cet état que j'appelais "la Suisse du Coeur."" (p. 118). Composite settings are used at times, as in *Villa triste* (Gallimard, 1975), where the spa town described, though conveniently close to the Swiss border, has overtones of Vichy. Another French setting, that of *Les Boulevards de ceinture,* is a small village close to the forest of Fontainebleau, a suitable place of refuge for a group of collaborators. In the only novel to be set entirely outside France, *Vestiaire de l'enfance* (Gallimard, 1989), to which I will return in more detail later, a composite country based on several Mediterranean locations is created. Escape to these places, however, always proves illusory, as the fear which haunts the protagonists is internal and cannot be eliminated by flight over boundaries.

Darrieussecq's border spaces include both the sea and unspecified but composite geographical locations, which contain elements of the Basque country and, like it, are close to the frontier. Darrieussecq's characters, like those of Duras, are irresistibly drawn to the sea, which is strongly present in all but her first novel. The forest, rather than the sea, features in *Truismes,* where the narrator retreats after her final metamorphosis into a sow. The composite location in which *Naissance des fantômes* is set bears some resemblance both to S. Tahla and to the town in which *Vestiaire de l'enfance* is set.

Transgression

Transgression is a major theme in Duras's novels. *L'Amante anglaise* (Gallimard, 1967) is entirely devoted to the exploration of the enigma posed by a particularly gratuitous murder and *Dix heures et demie du soir en été* (Gallimard, 1960) describes the aftermath of a *crime passionnel,* a subject already explored in *Moderato Cantabile.* Elsewhere, lesser criminal acts abound: as Victoria Best has observed,[10] the narrative of *Le Vice-consul* (Gallimard, 1965) is structured round a series of transgressions. The theme of sexual transgression recurs throughout Duras's work, from the adolescent's affair with the Chinese lover at the centre of *L'Amant* to the transgressional sexual behaviour of *La Maladie de la mort.* The crossing of boundaries implicit in the original meaning of the term transgression is encapsulated in the figure of the beggarwoman whose journey into madness holds a particular fascination for the author.

For Modiano, transgression precedes marginalization: it is the father's crime which has led to the son's alienation from his past and consequent exclusion from society. In the state of limbo to which he is condemned, the son seeks support and companionship, but as he is beyond the pale, he is doomed to fraternize with other marginalized people, many of whom have criminal associations. Alan Morris has usefully provided a list of these: " trafiquants du marché noir ... anciens et futurs détenus ... cambrioleurs ... receleurs ... voleurs ... racketteurs ... tortionnaires ... et assassins".[11] The criminal activities listed above are, of course, of the type which occurred frequently during the Occupation, so when they figure in Modiano's middle period novels, set mainly in the 1960s, there is a veiled allusion to the trangressive behaviour of the earlier period.

Two of Darrieussecq's protagonists are clearly transgressors: the main character in *Truismes*, who oversteps the bounds of decency and, towards the end of the novel, is an accomplice to murder, and the deserting wife in *Le Mal de mer*, who is described in the following terms by the detective: "Elle risque la prison pour soustraction d'enfant" (p. 109). The narrator of *Naissance des fantômes,* though not guilty of any criminal offence, can be seen as transgressing in the original sense of the term: she crosses over into a new dimension. In *Bref séjour chez les vivants*, the two sisters who were in charge of their brother when he drowned are perceived as responsible and thus transgressive by their father and their lives are blighted as a result of this guilt: one becomes mentally disturbed and the other flees to the other side of the world in an attempt to escape from her feelings of culpability, but finally meets a tragic end herself.

In the above brief outline, I have attempted to compare the nature and significance of the themes of marginalization and transgression in the novels of Duras, Modiano and Darrieussecq. While both themes are clearly present in the writing of all three authors, it is in Modiano's novels that they appear to me to be most strikingly in evidence: his narrators invariably suffer from a strong feeling of alienation linked with past transgression and make frequent reference to their marginalized state. I therefore propose to present a detailed analysis of one of his middle period novels, *Vestiaire de l'enfant*, as a study of extreme marginalization induced by transgression.

Vestiaire de l'enfance: marginalization induced by transgression

Vestiaire de l'enfance was published in 1989, just before Modiano returned to the period of the Occupation in *Voyage de noces*. There has been a tendency among critics to consider the novels of Modiano's middle period as being less interesting than those of his two trilogies: Ora

Avni is dismissive of them, criticising them for being deprived of a historical context,[12] while Alan Morris sees the break with the past ushered in by *Une Jeunesse* (Gallimard, 1981) as a change for the worse in Modiano's writing.[13] To my mind, however, these novels paint a powerful picture of the paralysis and mental anguish which result from marginalization. *Vestiaire de l'enfance*, which is pervaded by an atmosphere of profound alienation, is perhaps the most striking example in Modiano's *oeuvre* of the crippling effect of a refusal to confront the past.

The plot of *Vestiaire de l'enfance* is slight: a French author, Jimmy Sarano, is living in an unspecified Mediterranean location, having left France in mysterious circumstances, which necessitated changing his name. He has abandoned writing novels and now earns his living by churning out a radio serial of little worth. The tedium of his existence is temporarily relieved when he meets a girl who reminds him of a childhood friend. During his brief relationship with the girl, Marie, he returns in memory to the Paris of his youth and revisits past events of his adolescence. The relationship fails to prosper, however, and the putative identification between Marie and the childhood acquaintance is not authenticated. The novel ends, as it has begun, in an atmosphere of emptiness and silence.

As is invariably the case in Modiano's writing, transgression precedes marginalization, so I will first examine transgression in the novel before analysing its consequences. Transgression in *Vestiaire de l'enfance* is both individual and collective and is referred to obliquely. There are only two detailed references to the misdemeanour which caused the narrator to flee his native country, which occur respectively one-third and two-thirds of the way through the book. The first reference is particularly ambiguous: the narrator describes his permanent feelings of guilt as being connected with a recurring dream involving a car accident from which he escaped, abandoning his companion (p. 51). The second reference is more explicit: a French journalist, recognising him as the author Jean Moreno, challenges him in the following terms: " Je vais vous poser une question indiscrète … Vous étiez bien dans la voiture la nuit de l'accident? (…) C'était un crime ou tout simplement un cas banal de non-assistance à personne en danger ?" (p. 98). The narrator silences the journalist before giving him the slip, so the act of transgression remains enigmatic. Whatever its nature, however, it has had a devastating effect on its perpetrator, who as a consequence is living as an exile under an assumed name, in constant fear of exposure.

A clear link is made by the narrator between his own transgression and subsequent marginalization and that of his many compatriots who have also fled to the town where he lives. They too are described as exiles who are "en fin de parcours" (p. 36). Although they, unlike the narrator, have kept their real names, there is a feeling of solidarity between them and him: "nous sommes tous dans le même bain" (p. 50). Together they form a sort of Foreign Legion, linked by a vow of silence: "Le silence, voilà le seul moyen de tenir le coup. Le silence et l'amnésie"(p. 129). The reference to the Occupation is unmistakeable here, so it becomes clear that the transgression at the heart of the novel is that encapsulated in Henri Rousso's Vichy Syndrome,[14] in which the extent of French collaboration with the Vichy regime was denied by a significant element of the population in postwar France. The place to which the protagonists of the novel have fled can be equated with this realm of denial and refusal to confront the past.

The effect of Jimmy Sarano's refusal to face up to his past is marginalization leading to a state bordering on stasis. Condemned to live out his days in a foreign country, he can look forward to nothing but boredom and solitude: "Les jours succéderaient aux jours, monotones" (p. 20). In his exile it seems to him that time has come to a standstill: "Ici je suis arrivé au bout du monde et le temps s'est arrêté" (p. 24). Having abandoned his career as a novelist, he ekes out a living by writing a repetitive radio serial, whose subject, tellingly, is "la survie des personnes disparues" (p. 12). He compensates vicariously for his lost career by compulsively spying on an elderly neighbour, who, in a curious *dédoublement* of the narrator, is himself a successful author with many titles to his credit. This elderly author arouses such a strong feeling of loathing in the narrator that he contemplates murdering him: "Je ferais semblant de nettoyer une arme à feu et le coup partirait" (p. 69), but rejects this course of action as too risky. Here, marginalization caused by transgression is in danger of engendering further transgression. Jimmy Sarano lives in a constant state of fear that his real identity will be discovered: "je craignais de me retrouver en présence des gens que j'avais connus à Paris. Il est désagréable de nier sa propre identité" (p. 54). In this limbo-like existence, he is unable to make close friends: "Je n'ai pas lié de réelles amitiés" (p. 49) and is overwhelmed by: "une sensation de vide" (p. 31).   References to absence and emptiness punctuate the novel and these emotions threaten to engulf him (p. 101). Only by clinging to his false identity can he keep them at bay. But in doing so, he is doomed to an existence where repetition and circularity rather than progression prevail: "J'avais l'impression de revivre la même scène. J'étais revenu en arrière dans le temps" (p. 35). He and his compatriots end up by questioning their own identity and reality : "On finit par douter de sa langue maternelle et de sa propre existence" as well as the purpose of their lives : "On se demande à quoi servent toutes ces émissions que personne n'écoute"(p. 133).

The only escape from this bleak existence appears to lie in making contact with the past. In a second radio programme, transmitted at dead of night and known as *Appels dans la nuit*, Jimmy tries to make contact with his Parisian past by broadcasting messages based on information he has gleaned from old newspaper cuttings. These messages have overtones of the coded messages used by the Resistance in wartime France. After returning in memory to his adolescence in Paris, Jimmy briefly abandons his serial in order to write up his memories and breaks with his normal routine, experiencing as a result: "une sensation de légèreté, comme après avoir rompu une dernière entrave" (p. 135). By the end of the novel, however, after Marie's disappearance, he resumes his former activities and is once more engulfed by emptiness and silence (p. 151).

I will conclude this analysis of marginalization and transgression in *Vestiaire de l'enfance* with a brief examination of the liminal zone which Jimmy and his compatriots have chosen as their place of exile. Its exact location is left deliberately vague ; even those who live there have doubts about its existence : "On finit par douter de la réalité de cette ville et par se demander où elle se trouve exactement sur la carte : Espagne ? Afrique ? Méditerranée ?" (p. 133). As such, it is typical of Modiano's places of refuge, which, as we have seen, are more mental than physical. There is a fusion not only between different places: Paris, the Côte d'Azur, Spain and North Africa but also between different times: Marie's hotel room recalls the Paris hotel room to which the narrator returns in memory when reliving his adolescence. There is a thematic link between the call from the muezzin (p. 130) and the radio programme *Appels dans la nuit*. References to the statue of the local hero are clearly metaphorical in nature: the statue, perceived as protective by the narrator, moves from plinth to plinth and its pointing finger changes direction (p. 100), symbolising the narrator's displacement and lack of fixity. The town in which *Vestiaire de l'enfance* is set is the most sustained example of a composite location to be found in Modiano's novels. It gives refuge to those fleeing their past, but can also be seen as a place (or state) of transit: only by moving beyond its shelter will they be able to escape from marginality and re-enter the real world.

Conclusion

Vestiaire de l'enfance appears to me to be a prime example of a novel underpinned by the twin themes of marginalization and transgression. There is evidence on every page of the novel of the narrator's marginalization, which is a direct result of past transgression. As we have seen, this pattern of transgression followed by marginalization characterizes Modiano's work. As was demonstrated in earlier in this short article, Duras and Darrieussecq also make frequent references to marginalization and transgression throughout their writing, transgressive figures being particularly in evidence in Duras's novels. The twin themes are clearly linked to the three authors' major preoccupation, the search for identity in an unstable world. As part of this identity quest, considerations of inclusion and exclusion, of staying within boundaries, exploring them and going beyond them are of fundamental importance.

NOTES

[1] See M. Duras , *La Vie matérielle* (Gallimard, 1987), p. 78
[2] See C. Blot-Labarrère, *Marguerite Duras* (Seuil, 1992), p. 61
[3] See C. W. Nettelbeck and P. Hueston, *Patrick Modiano pièces d'identité: écrire l'entretemps* (Lettres Modernes, 1986), p. 5
[4] See J-L Ezine, *Les écrivains sur la sellette* (Seuil, 1981), p.22
[5] Ezine, *Les écrivains sur la sellette,* p. 22
[6] Each of the three writers lost a cherished brother
[7] See interview in *L'Humanité*, 13/09/01
[8] From interview in *Centre France – La Montagne* 8/03/98
[9] Defined as such by Baptiste Roux in *Figures de l'Occupation dans l'oeuvre de Patrick Modiano* (L'Harmattan, 1999), p. 11
[10] See V. Best , *Critical Subjectivities. Identity and Narrative in the Works of Colette and Marguerite Duras* (Peter Lang, 2000), p. 207

[11] See A. Morris , *Patrick Modiano* (Rodopi, 2000), p. 39
[12] See O. Avni , *D'un passé l'autre: aux portes de l'histoire avec Patrick Modiano* (L'Harmattan, 1977), p.151
[13] See A. Morris , *Patrick Modiano* (Berg, 1996), p. 107
[14] See H. Rousso , *Le syndrome de Vichy de 1944 à nos jours* (Seuil, 1987)